D1082505

SAUNDERS PHYSICAL ACTIVITIES SERIES

Edited by

MARYHELEN VANNIER, Ed.D.

Professor and Director, Women's Division
Department of Health and Physical Education
Southern Methodist University

and

HOLLIS F. FAIT, Ph.D.

Professor of Physical Education
School of Physical Education
University of Connecticut

GOLF

second edition

BILLYE ANN CHEATUM, Ph.D.

Associate Professor, Physical Education for Women
Western Michigan University

ILLUSTRATED BY JAMES BONNER

W. B. SAUNDERS COMPANY · PHILADELPHIA · LONDON · TORONTO

W. B. Saunders Company: West Washington Square
Philadelphia, Pa. 19105

12 Dyott Street
London, WC1A   1DB

833 Oxford Street
Toronto, Ontario M8Z 5T9, Canada

Saunders Physical Activities Series

Golf   ISBN 0-7216-2501-0

Last digit is the print number: 9   8   7   6   5   4   3   2

Editors' Foreword

Every period of history, as well as every society, has its own profile. Our own world of the last third of the twentieth century is no different. Whenever we step back to look at ourselves, we can see excellences and failings, strengths and weaknesses, that are peculiarly ours.

One of our strengths as a nation is that we are a sports-loving people. Today more persons — and not just young people — are playing, watching, listening to, and reading about sports and games. Those who enjoy themselves most are the men and women who actually *play* the game: the "doers."

You are reading this book now for either of two very good reasons. First, you want to learn — whether in a class or on your own — how to play a sport well, and you need clear, easy-to-follow instructions to develop the special skills involved. If you want to be a successful player, this book will be of much help to you.

Second, you may already have developed skill in this activity, but want to improve your performance through assessing your weaknesses and correcting your errors. You want to develop further the skills you have now and to learn and perfect additional ones. You realize that you will enjoy the activity even more if you know more about it.

In either case, this book can contribute greatly to your success. It offers "lessons" from a real professional: from an outstandingly successful coach, teacher, or performer. All the authors in the *Saunders Physical Activities Series* are experts and widely recognized in their specialized fields. Some have been members or coaches of teams of national prominence and Olympic fame.

This book, like the others in our Series, has been written to make it easy for you to help yourself to learn. The author and the editors want you to become more self-motivated and to gain a greater understanding of, appreciation for, and proficiency in the exciting world of *movement*. All the activities described in this Series — sports, games, dance, body conditioning, and weight and figure control activities — require skillful, efficient movement. That's what physical activity is all about. Each book contains descriptions and helpful tips about the nature, value, and purpose of an activity, about the purchase and care of equipment, and about the fundamentals of each movement skill involved. These books also tell you about common errors and how to avoid making them, about ways in which you can improve your performance, and about game rules and strategy, scoring, and special techniques. Above all, they should tell you how to get the most pleasure and benefit from the time you spend.

Our purpose is to make you a successful *participant* in this age of sports activities. If you are successful, you will participate often—and this will give you countless hours of creative and recreative fun. At the same time, you will become more physically fit.

"Physical fitness" is more than just a passing fad or a slogan. It is a condition of your body which determines how effectively you can perform your daily work and play and how well you can meet unexpected demands on your strength, your physical skills, and your endurance. How fit you are depends entirely on your participation in vigorous physical activity. Of course no one sports activity can provide the kind of total workout of the body required to achieve optimal fitness; but participation with vigor in any activity makes a significant contribution to this total. Consequently, the activity you will learn through reading this book can be extremely helpful to you in developing and maintaining physical fitness now and throughout the years to come.

These physiological benefits of physical activity are important beyond question. Still, the pure pleasure of participation in physical activity will probably provide your strongest motivation. The activities taught in this Series are *fun*, and they provide a most satisfying kind of recreation for your leisure hours. Also they offer you great personal satisfaction in achieving success in skillful performance—in the realization that you are able to control your body and its movement and to develop its power and beauty. Further, there can be a real sense of fulfillment in besting a skilled opponent or in exceeding a goal you have set for yourself. Even when you fall short of such triumphs, you can still find satisfaction in the effort you have made to meet a challenge. By participating in sports you can gain greater respect for yourself, for others, and for "the rules of the game." Your skills in leadership and fellowship will be sharpened and improved. Last, but hardly least, you will make new friends among others who enjoy sports activities, both as participants and as spectators.

We know you're going to enjoy this book. We hope that it—and the others in our Series—will make you a more skillful and more enthusiastic performer in all the activities you undertake.

Good luck!

MARYHELEN VANNIER
HOLLIS FAIT

Contents

5

6

1

Introduction

Golf is played on a course of nine or 18 holes, the distance between holes ranging from under 100 to over 500 yards. The golf ball is played from the teeing ground, an area near each hole designated by two markers. To play the ball with the club from this area a small object, called the tee, is used to elevate the ball. The well mowed areas between the holes are called fairways. Flanking the fairways are unkept areas of grass and trees, known as the rough, which, because of the hazard they present, increase the challenge of the game. Other hazards are waterholes and bunkers (mounds, sand traps and depressions on the fairway). The hole is located in an area of very short and carefully maintained grass called the green. The hole is actually a round cup, four and a half inches in diameter, set into the ground. Its location is marked by a removable flag. The object of the game is to play the ball from each tee to each hole of the course with the least number of strokes for a low total score.

Without question, golf is one of the most popular sports in the twentieth century. In 1973, alone, there were 804 new golf facilities under construction or opened for participation, bringing the total number of golf courses in the United States to 11,956. The facilities range from private to semiprivate, municipal, military, veterans', school and industrial. During 1973, there were approximately 13,550,000 golfers in the United States. The greatest surge of interest in purchasing golfing materals has occurred in the last twenty years. Since 1954, an average increase of $10,000,000 a year has been spent on golf bags, balls and clubs.

Golf instruction and equipment have never been better. Golf clubs have been improved to adequately match the shape, size, age and sex of the player. High speed photography has become a masterful teaching aid. The use of video tape immediately enables a golfer to see his swing as it really is and not the way he imagines it to be. Complimentary master clinics offered by the National Golf Foundation and the sporting goods' manufacturers reach thousands of people each year. The golf tournaments, available every weekend on television, as well as televised golf lessons, have had a tremendous influence on the promotion of golf.

Perhaps the intriguing element of golf lies in the challenge and the versatility of the game. There is no other sport in which you are able to compete with the proficient player and the least experienced player. Two players of varying degrees of ability are able to engage in an exciting, entertaining and closely matched game.

With the exception of the professionals, golf should be played for relaxation, recreation and enjoyment. Far too many people become overly concerned with their score and, thus, fail to enjoy the advantages of the game. Golf should afford you a release from the heavy pressures of your work and the fast pace of living and should offer you a chance to slow down and enjoy life.

It is necessary to attain a certain amount of skill in order to contact the ball and to play reasonably well. You are not a computerized machine, however, and should not expect to hit the ball perfectly every time or even the majority of the time. You will likely be a weekend golfer or will play only once or twice a week. It is as illogical to think that as a weekend golfer you can shoot par, as it is to think that you can play baseball with the major league teams or football with the professionals. In a way, watching the golf professionals on television is a little disheartening. The next time you play, you may feel despondent if you are unable to hit the ball as solidly as they do. You must remember that golf is their occupation; therefore, they spend as many or more hours playing and practicing golf as you do at your studies. You should be content to compete in such a manner as to present yourself with an enjoyable but challenging match.

Of greatest importance is the attitude you assume when approaching the task of learning the game of golf. You will need to be patient, open-minded, responsive to your instructor and willing to practice the seemingly simple techniques. As in all sports, you will reach a plateau. Along with increased determination and patience, your progression will depend upon your initial application of the basic fundamentals, your willingness to work on your game, and your ability to replace faulty habits with correct techniques.

HISTORY

The sport of golf, traceable to early historical times, originated when shepherds struck pebbles with their crooks, challenging each other both in distance and in aim. Caesar, utilizing a crooked stick and a leather ball packed with feathers, participated in a game called "Paganica" over two thousand years ago. During his conquest, Caesar,

with his legionnaires, spread the game of "Paganica" to many countries. As a result, the origin of the modern game of golf is highly controversial. Most historians, however, credit the development of the
sport to Scotland, Belgium or Holland, all of which have preserved
primary sources of data, proving that games closely resembling the
present day game of golf were played in the fourteenth and fifteenth
centuries.

Perhaps the most colorful stories of the early history of golf come
from Scotland, where the game was repeatedly banned by the royalty
in an attempt to preserve archery both as the national sport and as
the primary means of defense against their aggressive enemy, the
English.

The game of golf, as played in Scotland during the fourteenth
or early fifteenth century, consisted of "a leather bag stuffed with
feathers for a ball, and a club cut from a bent tree branch." Although
the growth of the game was slow at first, it gained such popularity in
the 1440's that King James II became alarmed that the skill of golf
would replace the skill of the bow and arrow. To preserve archery
competency in the citizen army, the Parliament of King James II
banned golf in 1457. Golf continued, however, to prosper and to interfere with archery to such a degree, that, in 1471, the Parliament of
James III issued a second act which stated that "Football and Golf
be utterly cryed down and not used." In spite of these two restrictions,
golf spread so rapidly throughout Scotland that, in 1491, the Parliament of James IV again prohibited the game of golf, this time im-
posing a fine and an imprisonment not only on the participants but
also on the owner of the property on which the game was being conducted. The war between Scotland and England ceased, in 1502, with
the signing of the treaty of perpetual peace by James IV of Scotland
and King Henry VII of England. With the subsequent marriage of
James IV to Princess Margaret, daughter of Henry VII, in 1503,
peace was assured between the two countries. This turn of events
enabled the Scots to disregard the injunctions against golf and openly
to pursue the game as their national sport.

King James IV of Scotland is recognized as the first member of
royalty to study seriously the game of golf. His granddaughter, Mary,
Queen of Scots, is recognized as history's first woman golfer. Queen
Mary, having received golf instruction during her childhood, both
encouraged golf and played openly, after her succession to the throne
in 1542. Praised as having skill "almost equal to men," the queen
brought scorn upon herself by playing golf a few days after the murder
of her ill-fated husband, Lord Darnley-Henry Stewart.

The origin of the term "caddie" is credited to Mary, Queen of
Scots. Educated in France, Mary engaged a French cadet to carry
her clubs. She referred to him as a "cadet," meaning someone who

is learning the game or who is a little chief, the title given to younger sons of French nobility who served as her pages. The French pronunciation of the word cadet was "cad-day," and the Scottish spelling of cadet was "caddie."

In 1552, during the reign of Queen Mary, the St. Andrews Golf Course, the most famous of all golf courses, was founded in St. Andrews, Scotland. On January 25, 1552, Archbishop John Hamilton granted a license to St. Andrews confirming the "rycht and possessioun, propirtie and communite of the saidis linkis in . . . playing at golff, futball, schuteing at all games with all other maner of pastime . . ." Subsequent ratifications were granted by Archbishop Gladstanes in 1614 and by James VI.

The first continuing golf course in the United States was founded, in 1888, by John Reid, a Scottish immigrant. Through the assistance of Robert Lockhart, a friend who was visiting in Scotland, Reid purchased his equipment from the St. Andrews Golf Course. On February 22, 1888, John Reid and John Upham played the first match over the new course. The course consisted of three short holes, with fairways approximately one hundred yards long, laid over a hilly pasture with cups scooped out of the ground. In 1889, John Reid and Miss Carrie Low succeeded in defeating Mrs. John Reid and John Upham in the first mixed foursome match.

The United States Golf Association was formed in 1894, as a result of a dispute over the United States Amateur Golf Champion. Two different clubs had sponsored Amateur Golf Championships with the emergence of two national champions. Realizing the need of a central governing body, five leading clubs formed the United States Golf Association to conduct championships, to establish rules and to develop the elements of sportsmanship in golf.

2

Equipment

Golfing equipment essential for playing the game consists of golf clubs, golf balls and tees and a bag to carry this equipment. A complete set of golf clubs includes fourteen clubs: four woods, eight irons, a wedge and a putter. Each club, designed for a specific purpose, is classified into woods, long irons, short irons and a putter. The golf industry offers a wide variety of clubs with numerous combinations of weight, shaft flexibility, length, grip and swing weight. Clubs that are an appropriate length and weight for you will mold your swing into an efficient pattern, whereas clubs that are not will exaggerate any errors in your swing. Your objective should be to find a set of golf clubs that will allow you to play to the best of your ability. In class you may do this through trial and error, with the clubs that are available to you. If you are purchasing clubs, seek the advice and assistance of a golf professional.

Golf balls are available in a wide range of prices. Those costing less do not generally perform as consistently or achieve as much distance as higher priced balls. The cheaper balls are usually adequate for practice, where distance is not of significance, and for beginning play on the course, when a number of balls will be lost. Balls that have been badly cut by the club in poor shots or have become water soaked do not perform well and should be discarded.

Tees are made of several kinds of material and their cost is determined by the quality of the material. Wood and plastic tees are the most commonly used; they are both serviceable and inexpensive.

Very serviceable, inexpensive bags may be purchased at discount stores. Lightweight canvas, plastic or vinyl bags with separate compartments for woods and irons are advisable if you plan to carry your own bag. If you hire a caddie, pull a golf cart or ride in a golf car, you may want to purchase a heavier, more expensive vinyl or leather bag.

THE CLUBS

Because of the importance of the clubs to the game, a detailed analysis of each kind of club is offered below.

5

The Woods

The woods are the longest and most powerful clubs in your bag. They usually include the driver (the number 1 wood), the number 2, 3, 4 and 5 woods. Since you are limited to fourteen total clubs, your set of woods will usually include three or four clubs. Beginners will often select the driver, the number 3 and the number 4 woods.

The Irons

Irons are classified according to their length and use as long irons, middle irons and short irons. The long irons (1, 2 and 3) are used for long approach shots to the green. The middle irons (4, 5 and 6) have a higher loft designed for approach shots to the green from a distance of 135 to 170 yards. The short irons (7, 8 and 9) are used for chipping and pitching as well as short accurate shots to the green. Advanced golfers will usually include the 2, 3, 4, 5, 6, 7, 8 and 9 irons in a set of clubs.

Putter

The putter is a short shafted, well balanced iron with a vertical face. It is used to stroke the ball into the hole from a position on the green or at the edge of the green.

Degree of Loft

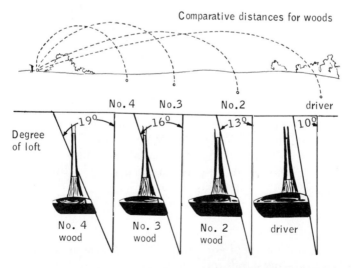

Comparative distances for woods

No. 4   No. 3   No.2   driver

Degree of loft   19°   16°   13°   10°

No. 4 wood   No. 3 wood   No. 2 wood   driver

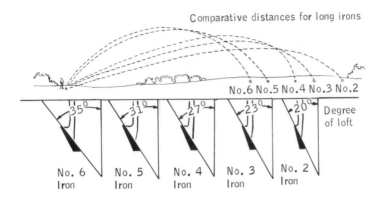

Comparative distances for long irons

No.6 No.5 No.4 No.3 No.2

35° 31° 27° 23° 20° Degree of loft

No. 6 Iron   No. 5 Iron   No. 4 Iron   No. 3 Iron   No. 2 Iron

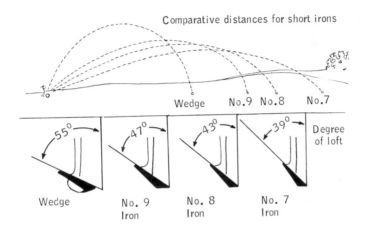

Comparative distances for short irons

Wedge   No.9 No.8   No.7

55° 47° 43° 39°   Degree of loft

Wedge   No. 9 Iron   No. 8 Iron   No. 7 Iron

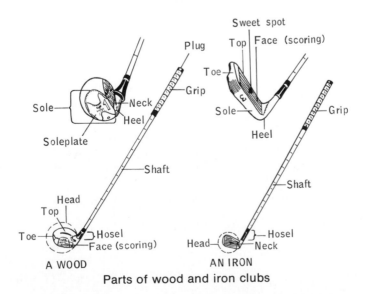

Sweet spot

Plug

Top | Face (scoring)

Toe

Sole — Neck
Heel

Soleplate

Grip

Sole   Heel

Grip

Shaft

Shaft

Head
Top

Toe — Hosel
Face (scoring)

Head — Hosel
Neck

A WOOD   AN IRON

Parts of wood and iron clubs

Special Clubs

The sand wedge is a short shafted, heavy iron designed to lift the ball from a sand trap or grass. The flange (base) of the sand wedge may be narrow, medium or wide. The wider the flange, the greater will be the bouncing quality of the club (see figure). If the ball is buried or in the heavy sand, the narrow and wide flanges are inadequate. For the greatest varieties of lies in the sand trap a medium flange offers the best performance.

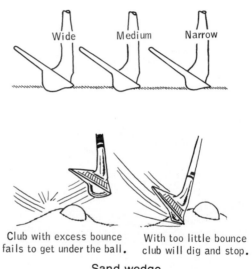

Club with excess bounce fails to get under the ball.　　With too little bounce club will dig and stop.

Sand wedge

Yardage of Clubs

When selecting your club for a particular shot, consider the weather and the condition of the fairway. When the weather is wet or humid, the flight of the ball will be less, therefore, add ten yards to your distance. Conversely, if the course is dry and the fairway has a hard surface, subtract ten yards from your distance. Hard surfaces will give your ball more roll whereas a soft fairway will stop the ball more abruptly.

Average distances for clubs are as follows (in yards):

CLUB	MEN	WOMEN
Driver	225−275	190−225
2 wood	215−235	190−210
3 wood	190−210	165−185

CLUB	MEN	WOMEN
4 wood	165 – 185	155 – 175
1 iron	190 – 210	160 – 180
2 iron	180 – 200	150 – 170
3 iron	170 – 190	140 – 160
4 iron	160 – 180	130 – 150
5 iron	150 – 170	120 – 140
6 iron	130 – 150	110 – 130
7 iron	110 – 130	90 – 110
8 iron	90 – 110	70 – 110
9 iron	90 – 120	60 – 90
Pitching wedge	70 – 90	50 – 90

Club	Type of Shot
Driver	From the tee for slow flat trajectory with maximum distance.
2 wood	From the tee when the wind is behind you and from the fairway when the ball has a good lie.
3 wood	By the average player for a long fairway shot from a good lie.
4 wood	For long shots when the ball is in heavy grass.
2 iron	For long fairway shots. Beginners should use a 3 wood instead of the 2 iron.
3 iron	For long fairway shots that do not require the distance of the 2 iron. Has more loft than number 2 iron and is easier to control.
4 iron	For lifting shots out of the rough as well as fairway shots of 130 – 180 yards. Short chip shots.
5 iron	Used on the fairway for shots of 120 – 170 yards. Chip and pitch and run approach shots.
6 iron	For approach shots. More loft than the 5 iron, thus ball will stop more abruptly. Short chip shots.
7 iron	For a lower flight with more roll than an 8 iron. Fairway shots of 90 – 130 yards, chip and pitch and run approach shots.
8 iron	For shots with a high trajectory and little roll. Pitch and run and pitch approach shots.
9 iron	For imparting the highest trajectory and the least amount of roll on the ball. Pitch shot when you wish the ball to stop suddenly.

ADDITIONAL EQUIPMENT

Optional equipment includes spiked golf shoes and gloves for one or both hands. For beginners, tennis shoes or flat street shoes are adequate, but since balance and rhythm are essential in a well co-ordinated golf swing, the balance obtained through the use of golf shoes is worth the investment of a few dollars. Players with small hands will find that a glove worn on the hand that is higher on the shaft or gloves on both hands will assist in maintaining a secure grip on the club.

CARE OF EQUIPMENT

Woods

Protect your woods from temperature and humidity by placing a head cover over each club. Avoid dropping your clubs on the ground. The irons may fall against the woods and leave indentations on the heads. When the surface of a wood is broken, the protective coating is cracked and subject to damage from moisture. After playing a round of golf, dry your woods and apply paste wax.

Irons

During a round of golf, use a wet towel or a golf tee to remove any dirt or grass that has accumulated in the grooves of your irons. The ball will not rebound off the clubface properly when the grooves are filled with dirt. After playing, clean the heads and the shafts with soap and water. Occasionally use a metal polish.

Grips

With repeated use, the grips will become slick. To restore tacki-ness to leather grips use an application of castor oil. Rubber grips may be cleaned with soap and water.

Shoes

Remove dirt, grass and stains from your shoes before storing them on a shoe tree. Occasionally polish them with a good conditioner. When the cleats on your shoes begin to wear, you may have them re-placed by the club professional for a small fee. For better balance, have all the cleats on both shoes replaced at the same time.

Bags

Recondition your bag with a leather conditioner twice a year. Do not sit on the front of your bag as this will destroy the rim and cause your clubs to hit against each other.

Balls

Balls will often become dirty during a round of golf. Cleaning equipment is usually located beside each teeing area. Avoid the use of a cleaner on the balls. To get maximum distance in cold weather, warm a ball in your pocket before hitting it. Store balls in a dark room with moderate temperature.

THE GOLF COURSE

The golf course usually consists of (1) a golf house or a country club, (2) a professional golf shop where equipment is sold and where you register to play, (3) a practice range, (4) a practice putting green

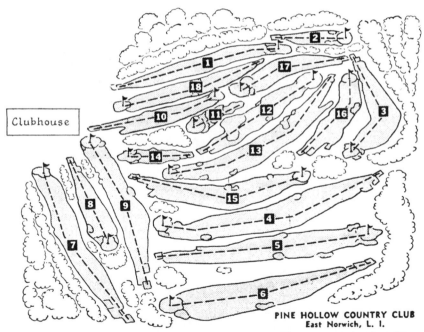

The layout of a typical 18 hole golf course. (© by The New York Times Company. Reprinted by permission.)

Hole	Yardage	Men's par	Women's par	Hole	Yardage	Men's par	Women's par
1	535	5	5	10	385	4	4
2	208	3	3	11	176	3	3
3	392	4	4	12	393	4	4
4	551	5	5	13	583	5	6
5	445	4	5	14	182	3	3
6	403	4	5	15	404	4	5
7	354	4	4	16	396	4	4
8	225	3	4	17	396	4	4
9	363	4	4	18	469	4	5

and (5) a nine or an 18 hole course. Each golf hole is ranked according to the distance from the teeing ground to the hole and is awarded a par figure. Par is the standard score established for the hole and the course.

U.S.G.A. Computation of Par

Par	Women	Men
3	0–210 yards	0–250 yards
4	211–400 yards	251–470 yards
5	401–575 yards	471 and over
6	576 and over	

3

Basic Skills

GRIP

The grip is the foundation of a good golf swing. It is your single connection with the golf club and thus affects the position of your clubhead throughout the swing and during impact. When your hands are not functioning properly, the arms, elbows, shoulders, body, legs and feet will not coordinate in the correct manner. Primarily you should select a grip which is comfortable to you and one which will permit your hands and wrists to work together as one unit. In this way you will achieve a free and uniform hand action throughout the swing while maintaining a square position of the club face at the top of your backswing and at your point of impact.

Hereafter, the descriptions are for the righthanded golfer. The three grips commonly used by most golfers are the Vardon (over-lapping), the ten finger and the interlocking. In all of these your hands are held close together, a half-inch from the head of the shaft, with the right hand secured below the left. The difference between the various grips involves the location of the little finger of your right hand. In the Vardon grip you place the little finger of the right hand over the left index finger; in the ten finger grip, your little finger is placed on the grip of the club just below the index finger of the left hand; and in the interlocking grip, your little finger is interlocked with the index finger of your left hand. As in the case of most players, you may find the Vardon grip, named after Harry Vardon, an English professional golfer who won the British open six times, more adaptable to your hand strength and size.

Vardon Grip

In the Vardon grip the handle of the club is held in the palm and fingers of the left hand and the fingers of the right hand, with the hands in a close, compact position.

To take the grip, hold the club in your right hand with the face of the club at a square position (right angle to your intended line of flight) and with the sole flat on the ground (see below). Place the shaft of your club diagonally across the palm and fingers of the left hand.

THE LIE OF THE CLUBHEAD

Sole flat on ground   Toe slightly off ground   Heel slightly off ground

The club should extend from below the first joint of the index finger to above the first joint of the little finger. There should be space for two fingers between the base of the hand and the end of the club.

If you are a beginner, practice assuming the grip with the club in the air as this is less difficult than when it is soled flat on the ground. After checking your grip, lower your club to the ground and place the sole in a flat position behind the ball.

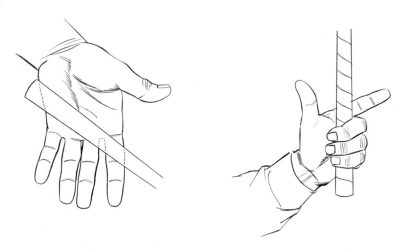

Close your fingers around the shaft with the last three fingers of the left hand maintaining a firm grip on the shaft. The index finger circles the club and almost touches the thumb. If you will concentrate on keeping the little finger of the left hand firm, the next two fingers will tend to hold firmly also. A good way to practice this is to hold the club with just the last three fingers of the left hand. Move the club from a parallel position with the ground to a vertical position by flexing your wrists. No space should be visible between the little finger and the shaft of the club.

The left thumb is placed on the right of the center of the shaft. Avoid a long thumb position; make sure that your thumb is not extending beyond your index finger. Keep the back of your left hand parallel to the club and perpendicular to an imaginary line drawn from the ball to the target. When looking down, you should see two and a half to three knuckles of the left hand. The large V formed by the thumb and index finger should be pointing just to the inside of the right shoulder.

Hold the club with your proper left hand grip and place the right hand against the club just below the left. Keep the palm of your right hand parallel to the shaft and to your intended target.

r right hand around the shaft with the left thumb snugly cup of the right palm.

Place the thumb in a natural position to the left of the center of the shaft with your right thumb and index finger as close together as possible. As you look down on the hands, the knuckles of the first two fingers should be showing.

Curl your little finger over your left index finger. You may find it more comfortable to rest the little finger in the space between the first two knuckles of the left hand.

Control the right hand's grip with the middle two fingers of your right hand. As you look down, the closed V formed by the thumb and forefinger should point to the inside of your right shoulder.

Check points for Vardon grip

LEFT HAND

1. Club lies diagonally across your palm and rests against the middle joint of your left hand.
2. Space for two fingers between base of your left hand and end of club.
3. Thumb of your left hand is located slightly to the right of the center of the shaft and exerts a gripping pressure.
4. When your finger and palm are closed on the shaft, the line formed by the thumb and index finger of the left hand should point just inside the right shoulder.
5. Knuckles of your first two and one-half or three fingers can be seen.
6. Index finger circles around the club and almost touches your thumb. (Depends on the size and length of your fingers.)
7. Last three fingers of your left hand maintain grip pressure.

RIGHT HAND

1. Little finger of your right hand rests in the groove between the first and second fingers of your left hand.
2. Line formed by thumb and index finger will point toward the area just inside of your right shoulder.
3. Knuckles of your first two fingers can be seen.
4. Thumb meets your index finger just to the left of the center of the shaft.
5. Palm of your right hand faces squarely toward the target.
6. Thumb of your left hand fits snugly into the hollow of your right palm.
7. There should be no gap or space showing between your two hands or between the thumb and index finger of both hands.
8. Middle two fingers and thumb maintain the grip, not the palm.

Looking down on grip to check it

Interlocking Grip

The interlocking grip is designed for those who have small hands, who lack strength or who have difficulty maintaining the Vardon grip.

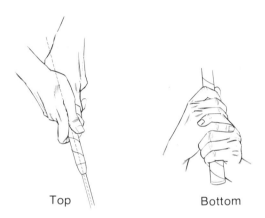

Top   Bottom

Interlocking grip viewed from top and bottom

By interlocking the little finger of your right hand with the index finger of your left hand, you will have a firm grip on the club and more confidence throughout your swing. Even though most instructors and students use the Vardon grip, you should not be ashamed of using the interlocking grip. Your purpose, after all, is to get the ball into the hole and professional golfers, such as Jack Nicklaus, who won $188,998.08 in prize money, in 1967, and Gene Sarazen find the inter- locking grip most beneficial.

Ten Finger Grip

In the ten finger grip, place your hands in the same relative posi- tion as in the Vardon or the interlocking grip but do not let your right little finger overlap or interlock with your left index finger. The hands remain close together with your right little finger placed on the shaft next to the left index finger. With ten fingers on the club, you will have a tendency to palm the club instead of maintaining a finger grip.

If you use this grip, it would be interesting for you to observe golf professionals, Art Wall and Bob Rosburg, who often play on television and are advocates of the ten finger grip.

Errors in the Grip

Error: Palming the club in the left hand.
Result: There will be no finger action of the left hand.
Correction: Check to be sure that the head of the shaft is located at the base of the fingers, not at the base of the thumb. Hold the club with the palm and the fingers of the left hand. The fingers press the handle toward the palm.

Error: Loose grip at the top of your backswing.
Result: The ball flight will be inconsistent.
Correction: Make sure the last three fingers of your left hand do not release the club. With a firm left hand grip, there should be no space visible between the shaft of the club and your fingers at the top of your backswing.

Correct left hand grip at the top of the backswing. Your last three fingers make a firm coupling with the club.

Loose grip at the top of your backswing will cause you to hit inconsistently.

Error: Long left thumb.

Result: A smothered shot. The long left thumb produces a loose grip at the top of the backswing which forces you to hit from the top of the backswing.

Correction: Pull the thumb up at least a half inch with the pad of the thumb pressed against the shaft of the club.

Right hand grip too far to the left—slice

Left hand grip too far to the left—slice

Error: Hands are placed too far to the left on the shaft.
Result: The face of the club will be open at top of the backswing
    and at the point of impact. The ball will slice (curve to the right
    in flight).
Correction: Take proper grip. The closed V's formed by the
    thumbs and the index fingers point just inside of your right
    shoulder.

Error: Hands too far to right on shaft.
Result: The left hand is on top of the shaft and the right hand is
    under the shaft. The face of the club will be closed at the top of
    your backswing and at the point of impact. The ball will hook
    (curve to the left in flight), or result in a smothered shot (driven
    into the ground).
Correction: The closed V's formed by the thumbs and the index
    fingers point just inside of your right shoulder.

Right hand grip too far to the right—hook

Left hand grip too far to the right—hook

Practice hints for the grip

1. To determine if you are holding the club in the palm and fingers of the left hand, grip the club in the address position. Take your right hand off the club and turn the left hand until the palm is facing directly toward the sky. Raise the club to a parallel position with the ground. Now, grasp the shaft with your right hand and open the fingers of the left hand. If you have a palm and finger grip, there will be space between the shaft of the club and your fingers.

2. Those of you who are having difficulty assuming the proper grip may place the sole of the club flat on the ground, with the head of the shaft resting against your belt. Drop the hands and extend them toward the shaft keeping the palm of each hand parallel to the shaft. Place the hands on the shaft in your preferred grip. When you have completed the grip, the palms of the hands should still be facing each other and be parallel to the shaft.

3. The shaking hands method of gripping the club may help you to assume the proper grip. Shake left hands with a partner, then drop your hand from that position and place it on the club in a similar manner. Repeat the same procedure with your right hand.

4. You may prefer the pistol shooting method of gripping the club. In this method, position your left hand as if you were shooting a pistol, then place the hand on the club in the same manner. Repeat the shooting action with your right hand and place it on the club.

5. Although the club must be held firmly, the forearm should not be unduly tense. Take your left hand grip and hold the club parallel to the ground and toward your partner. As he pulls on the end of the club, your arms move forward with the action but the club remains in your hand. Your partner should not be able to feel a strong resistance. If your grip is too strong, relax it slowly until your partner gently

removes the club from your hand. Then tighten your grip until you are able to hold the club and still respond to his pull. Next, have your partner turn the clubhead to the left and to the right. Respond with the degree of control that will enable you to maintain a relaxed but firm grip, while preventing the clubhead from turning.

THE SWING

There are as many styles of swinging the golf club as there are players. Basically, the golf swing is the synchronization of the grip, the address and the swing to impart maximal force upon the ball at the moment of impact. The distance a ball travels is determined by the speed of your clubhead at the moment of impact. Not to be confused with a fast swing, speed of the clubhead refers to the momentum created through a rhythmical well controlled swing. No effort should be made, either by acceleration or deceleration, to interrupt the natural momentum of your swing. Simply concentrate on a smooth backswing, downswing and follow-through.

Although each one of you will develop personal idiosyncrasies, basic fundamentals will be remarkably similar. These can be narrowed down into (1) good balance, (2) good rhythm, (3) unified backswing, (4) hips turning first on your downswing and (5) square position of your clubhead at address, halfway through your backswing, top of your backswing, halfway through your downswing, impact and halfway through your follow-through.

Preparation Techniques for the Golf Swing

The length of your arc and your control over the club will range from the 9 iron, the shortest and easiest club to swing, to the driver, one of the most difficult clubs in your set. As the clubs decrease in number, the length of your backswing and follow-through will increase. For this reason, it is wise to begin your first golf lesson with a chip shot. There are, however, certain preparation techniques which will develop a judgment of the distance to the hole and a feeling for the swing. Prior to your first lesson, participate in a few golf exercises.

1. To develop a sense of feeling for the swing and a judgment of your distance from the hole, stand at the edge of the green and toss a ball toward the hole. Use an underhand swing and let the ball roll off your fingertips. Repeat several times; then at the edge of the green take a square stance (see p. 26) with the cup as the target. Toss the

ball toward the hole with the right arm executing a short backswing, downswing and follow-through.

2. Take your proper grip and practice swinging the club back and forth over a path six inches to either side of the center of your feet. Gradually increase the length of your backswing and the length of your follow-through. Keep the swinging motion confined to your arms and hands. Check the relationship of your hands to the clubhead throughout the motion.

3. Another way to develop a swinging action is to pretend that you are using your club to cut weeds. With your correct grip, rhythmically swing your club back and forth in tall grass or weeds. Concentrate on keeping the club in contact with the grass as long as possible on both the backswing and the follow-through.

Stance

The posture and alignment assumed as you address the ball directly affect the plane of your swing and the path of your clubhead. Alignment governs your ability to turn properly, to shift weight, and to retain balance during your swing. The type of stance you take, therefore, should provide a balanced comfortable position with a good firm footing.

The three positions of the feet used when hitting a ball include the square, the open and the closed. The one you select will depend upon the club you choose, the type of shot you want to hit and the lie of the ball. Until you become a more experienced golfer, you will be wise to select the square stance and to use it with all of your clubs and your shots. The intricacies of the grip and the swing present an ample challenge to any beginner without increasing the margin of error by moving the feet, as required by the other stances.

Square stance

To assume the square stance, sight the intended line of flight of your ball (draw an imaginary line through the ball to the target). The face of your clubhead is placed behind the ball in a square position (right angle to the intended line of flight). Place yourself behind the ball in such a way as to position your feet on a line parallel to your line of flight. Your feet should be turned slightly outward with your hips, knees and shoulders also parallel to the intended flight of your ball. The square stance is generally used with the middle irons (4, 5 and 6); however, some players prefer to use the square stance with the long irons (2 and 3) as well as the middle irons.

Square stance

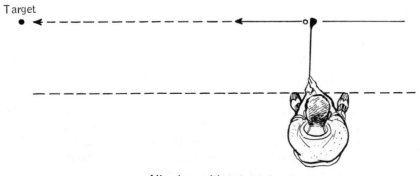

Target

Aligning with a target

Target

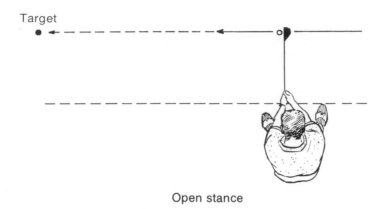

Open stance

Open stance

In the open stance you assume the same position as in the square stance but drop the left foot slightly back from the line of flight. This opens (or turns) your body toward your intended line of play. Since your hips are turned toward the target, your body rotation will be more fluid during your follow-through but somewhat limited during your backswing. In this position, your arms remain closer to the body for a more compact stroke. The open stance should be used with your short irons (7, 8, 9) for chipping and pitching. Since these are approach shots to the green, accuracy, not distance, is your main objective. When you open your stance, you deliberately block your right side, forcing a shorter, more compact and thus, more accurate shot.

Open stance—side view

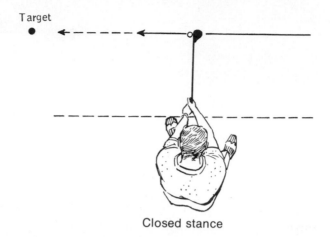

Target

Closed stance

Closed stance

In the closed stance you assume the same position as you did in the square stance but drop your right foot slightly back from the line of flight. Consequently, your hips are slightly turned toward your backswing. This positions your body for a more fluid movement or rotation during your backswing but restricts your follow-through. Generally speaking, you should use the closed stance when you wish to hit the ball a greater distance such as in your drive or in your long fairway shots (2 and 3 irons and all woods).

Closed stance—side view

DETAILED PICTORIAL VIEW OF THE SQUARE STANCE

Position of feet: Stand behind your ball and mentally draw a line through the ball to your target. To save time, sight your target and line of play as you approach a fairway shot.

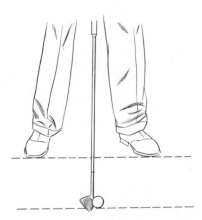

Place your feet on a line parallel to your line of flight. Weight is evenly distributed between both feet, with the weight of each foot located between the ball of your foot and the heel.

PLACEMENT OF FEET IN RELATION TO THE CLUB

For a wood shot spread your feet shoulder width apart. Weight should be evenly divided between your feet and carried back toward your heels.

As you progress from the woods to the short iron, your feet move closer together.

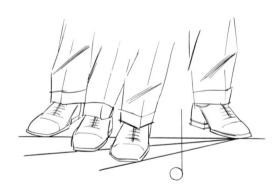

Address

Position of body at address

Flex your knees and hips slightly while pressing the right knee toward your left. You may feel a pushing sensation with the inner edge of the right foot. Keep the back straight, incline your body slightly forward from the hips. Your left arm should be straight while your right elbow is bent slightly toward the body and in line with the right knee.

Position of the sole of the club

At address, place the sole of your club flat on the ground behind the ball. The center of your clubhead should be directly behind the ball in line with your intended line of flight.

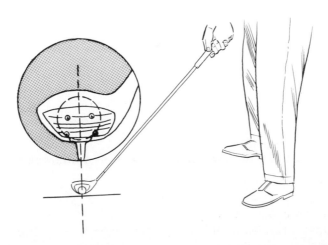

Position of hand and clubs in relation to ball

Your position in relation to the ball varies with each club. Since your distance from the ball varies with each club, apply this test to determine if you are standing correctly. Place the fingers of your right hand in the space between your leg and the top of your club. Your fingers should fit comfortably within this area.

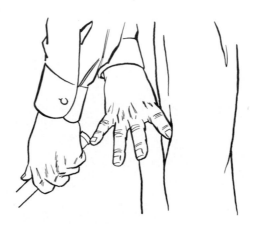

Position of the ball will vary from the inside of your left heel for the drives to the middle of your feet for the short irons.

Major check points for square stance and address position

1. Feet on a line parallel with your target.
2. Distance between feet appropriate for club and shot.
3. Weight balanced over both feet.
4. Hips and knees slightly flexed with your back inclined forward.

5. Right knee pressing toward left.

6. Distance between legs and top of your club should equal the spread of your fingers.

7. Ball placed within the area from the center of your feet for the short iron to the left heel for the driver.

8. Sole of your club resting flat on the ground with the center of the clubface directly behind the ball.

Position of ball in relation to stance and club

Your address in relation to the ball will be determined by the type of shot you wish to hit and the club you select. When your club contacts the ball at the center of the bottom arc of your downswing, the ball will get the proper loft for which the clubhead was designed. Each club, by virtue of the angle of the face and the composition of the head, is designed for a particular purpose.

Practice hints for square stance and address position

While approaching the ball, mentally draw an imaginary line from the ball to the target. Sight a second line that extends from your ball to an object on the right side of the fairway. The second line should be perpendicular to the target line. As you address the ball, assume a square position facing the object on the right side of the fairway. You will automatically be aligned correctly.

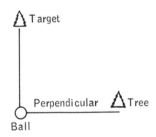

While practicing, periodically place a club across your toes. Step back and see if that line is parallel to your line of flight. Change targets on the practice range and experiment with changing your stance in relation to the new targets.

To further insure a square stance, place a second club behind the ball parallel to your target line. These two clubs should be in a square position toward each other. Often, it helps to place a third club or a piece of string between the first two clubs and perpendicular to the line of flight.

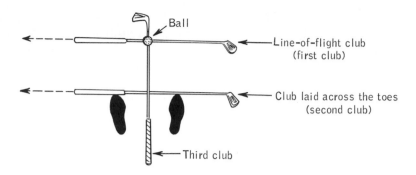

Ball

Line-of-flight club
(first club)

Club laid across the toes
(second club)

Third club

If you have difficulty in keeping a mental picture of your line of flight and target, stand behind the ball and determine your target. Draw an imaginary line from your ball to the target. Now locate an object such as a twig, blade of grass, or rough spot on the ground that is a few inches in front of your ball and in line with the target and the ball. By positioning yourself correctly in relation to this object, you will be aiming toward your target. While practicing, instead of using an object such as grass or twigs, substitute a more obvious target such as a golf tee or a club.

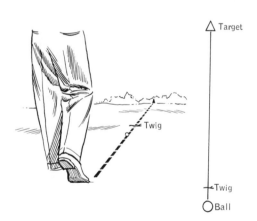

Target

Twig

Twig

Ball

The Waggle

The waggle is a series of movements of the clubhead forward and backward before hitting the ball. These movements are used to release tension which allows you to have a smooth, rhythmical swing. The waggle is an individual matter, performed differently by each player.

Pattern for developing a waggle

1. Address your ball the same way each time.
2. Walk up to the ball and set your grip.
3. Take your stance.
4. Waggle.

The Forward Press

The forward press is a slight shifting of your weight to the left in preparation for the swing. As soon as you complete your waggle, execute the forward press to break tension and to initiate a smooth takeaway. Work on developing a forward press that blends into your pre-swing pattern and avoid imitating the style of other players.

Examples of the forward press:

1. Pressing your right knee toward your left knee.
2. Turning your left hip slightly to the left.
3. Pressing forward an inch or so with your hands.
4. Pressing down with the instep of your right foot.

The Chip Shot

The chip shot is an approach shot to the green which has a low flight and rolls to the cup. Most frequently the chip shot is used with the 5, 6, 7, 8 or 9 iron when the green is open and there is no hazard between your ball and the green. Select the appropriate club according to your distance from the edge of the green, the lie of the ball, and the distance you want the ball to roll. Generally you should take the club with the least loft that will place the ball onto the green and let it roll into the cup. Start your first practice of the chip shot with a short iron, preferably the 9 iron. Use no body motion or transfer of weight and just enough hand and arm action to give you a slow, smooth, effortless swing.

Address

Take your grip lower on the shaft than for the drive. Keep your head over the ball and your body as motionless as possible. Your target line extends from the pin to the ball. Place your feet close together in a square stance with your weight slightly on the left foot. The ball is played on a line midway between your feet.

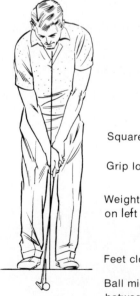

Square stance

Grip low on shaft

Weight a little
on left foot

Feet close together

Ball midway
between feet

Using only your hands and forearm, press the club slowly back to a square position a foot or two from the ground.

Contact the ball with your clubhead in a square position and your right palm facing the target. Maintain your head position over the ball until after the ball leaves the ground.

Follow-through will be short with the face of your club remaining square.

Check points for chip shots

1. Feet close together in a square stance.
2. Weight slightly on the left foot.
3. Ball is played on a line midway between your feet.
4. Hand and forearm action.
5. Clubhead square on the backswing, impact and follow-through.
6. Head remains over the ball until the ball has been hit.
7. Swing is a slow, smooth, effortless action.

Specific Clubs

Short irons (7-8-9)

Assume your square stance (when you become more proficient use an open stance), with your feet close together. Weight is balanced between the heels and the balls of your feet. The right knee is pressing in toward the left. The ball is played midway between your feet.

Start the backswing with your shoulders, arms, hands and hips moving simultaneously in a smooth rhythmical movement.

Shift your weight toward the right foot. As your club reaches a parallel position to the ground, your clubhead should be square.

Break your wrist approximately waist high. Your left arm remains extended while your right arm bends. The club will not reach a horizontal position. Hips and shoulders will turn in relation to the height of your backswing. (Remember you are striving for accuracy, not distance.)

Top of backswing

Pull the clubhead down with your left arm while the right elbow stays close to your body. As the arms start down, transfer your weight toward the left foot.

Your eyes remain on the ball until it leaves the ground. At the moment of impact your clubhead is in a square position toward your target.

Keep your clubhead low as long as possible on your follow-through. Concentrate on swinging through the ball. (The tendency is to quit once you contact the ball.)

Check points for short irons
Stance
1. Square stance.
2. Weight balanced between heels and balls of your feet.
3. Right knee pressing toward left.
4. Ball played midway between your feet.

Backswing
1. Unified backswing of hands, arms, hips and shoulders.
2. Weight transfers toward right foot.
3. Wrists unlock as your hands pass waist level.
4. Left arm remains extended, right arm bends.
5. Club reaches approximately a perpendicular position to the ground.

Downswing
1. Hips initiate downswing.
2. Pull clubhead down with left arm.

3. Right arm stays close to body.
4. Transfer weight toward left foot.
5. Clubhead is in a square position at the moment of impact.
Follow-through
1. Swing through ball keeping the clubhead low as long as possible.
2. Transfer weight to left foot.

Middle irons (4-5-6)

Take a square stance with your weight evenly distributed over both feet. Place the ball to the left of the center of your stance.

Start your backswing in the same manner as you did with the short irons. There should be unified movement of your hands, arms, shoulders and hips.

Your left arm and the club form a straight line until the club passes your waist. Transfer your weight slowly to the inside of your right foot.

As you reach the top of the backswing, your shoulders will turn to the right with your left shoulder under the chin. The club is not in a horizontal position; however, both hands are under the shaft.

Pull the left arm down so the grip end of the club points first toward the ground and then the ball. Start your downswing by turning your hips and transferring your weight toward the left foot. Keep your head in a steady position over the ball, your left arm straight, and your right elbow close to your body.

As your hands near your body, unlock your wrists. Guide the club with your left arm and hand. Let the right hand whip through the center of your downswing.

After hitting the ball, continue to look at the spot where the ball was placed. Fully extend the right arm toward your line of flight.

As you complete the follow-through, transfer your weight to the left foot. Your hands should be high, the left elbow bent and pointing to the ground, and your right shoulder under your chin.

CHECK POINTS FOR MIDDLE IRONS
Stance
1. Square stance.
2. Ball played to the left of the center of your stance.
Backswing
1. Unified movement of hands, arms, legs and shoulders.
2. Weight transfers to the inside of your right foot.
3. Left shoulder under your chin at top of backswing.
4. Club not in a horizontal position to ground.
Downswing
1. Initiated by hips.
2. Weight transfers to left foot.
3. Head in a steady position over the ball.
4. As your hands pass waist level, right hand whips through center of downswing.
Follow-through
1. Extend right arm toward aim of flight.
2. Transfer weight to left foot.
3. Right shoulder under chin at top of follow-through.

Long irons (2-3)

After you have learned to control the middle irons, the long irons will not present too many changes. Essentially the main difference will be the horizontal position of the club at the height of your back-

ADDITIONAL CHECK POINTS FOR LONG IRONS
1. Square stance (or slightly closed).
2. Weight evenly distributed on both feet.
3. Toes pointing straight ahead or pointing out slightly.
4. Ball played two or three inches in from left heel.

swing. This position of the club will allow you to have a greater arc
to your swing and thus more momentum at impact. The hips and
shoulders will rotate more on your backswing and on the follow-
through.

Full swing

Stance

Halfway through backswing

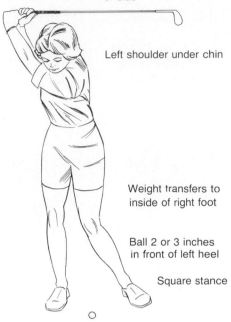

Horizontal position
of club

Left shoulder under chin

Weight transfers to
inside of right foot

Ball 2 or 3 inches
in front of left heel

Square stance

Top of backswing

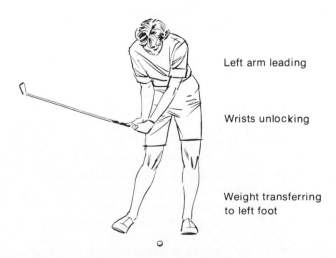

Left arm leading

Wrists unlocking

Weight transferring
to left foot

Halfway through downswing

Elbows in same
position as address

Weight more on
left foot

Clubhead square

Impact

Fairway woods (2-3-4)

Distance is achieved with the fairway woods by using a full swing. The stroke is executed exactly as it is in using the long irons.

The selection of your fairway wood will be determined by the loft of the club, the lie of your ball and the distance from the hole. The higher the number of the wood, the more loft the club will have. Select the number 2 fairway wood when the ball is in a relatively good lie and you wish to gain as much distance as possible. When the lie is good, use a 3 wood with the ball played off the heel of your left foot. If the ball is in a snug situation, use a 4 wood. With the 4 wood, play the ball approximately an inch away from your left heel, the clubhead will then meet the ball coming into the arc of your downswing. Concentration should be placed on a sweeping action of your clubhead which will allow the loft of the club to lift the ball into the air. Stronger people with a well coordinated swing may use woods in short rough. If there is any doubt in your mind concerning your ability to lift the ball out of the lie with a wood, use an iron.

ADDITIONAL CHECK POINTS FOR FAIRWAY WOODS
1. Square stance (or slightly closed).
2. Ball slightly behind left heel.
3. Weight evenly distributed over both feet.
4. Club will reach horizontal position on backswing.

Driver (1)

The object of the drive is to keep the ball in flight as long as possible and to position the ball for an easy second shot onto the putting green. The stroke is like that used for the other woods with the club in a horizontal position on the backswing. Strive for maximal efficiency on the drive, but do not change the rhythm of the stroke. While you are in the process of learning the drive, you may wish to use the 2 or 3 wood off the tee.

ADDITIONAL CHECK POINTS FOR DRIVE
1. Square stance or a slightly closed stance.
2. Ball opposite left heel.
3. Weight evenly distributed over both feet.
4. Club will reach a horizontal position on your backswing.

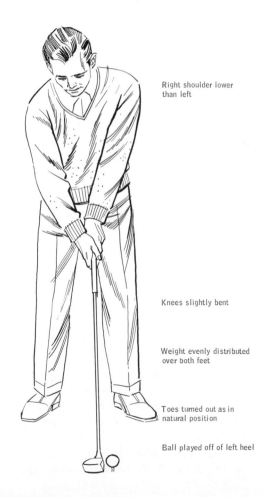

Right shoulder lower than left

Knees slightly bent

Weight evenly distributed over both feet

Toes turned out as in natural position

Ball played off of left heel

Errors

While it is important to develop a well coordinated stroke, the proficient golfer also must have the ability to isolate and to correct errors. However vague or small, there is a reason for every bad shot. Usually you can go back to your basic fundamentals and locate the problem in your grip, stance or address position. If these seem correct, then analyze the backswing, the top of the backswing, the downswing and the impact position. If there is no instructor or golf professional available to assist you, assess your own mistake and follow the instructions for correcting it. Try only one remedy at a time.

Error: Slicing

Result: The clubhead contacts the ball with an open face sending
   your ball on a curved flight to the right.
Correction:

The clubface is open. The line indicates where your clubface should be.

1. Hand position may have changed. Make sure two and a half to three knuckles of your left hand are showing. Closed V's, formed by your thumbs and index fingers, should point just inside of the right shoulder (see page 53).
2. Club position at address may be open. Place the face of the club square to the intended flight of your ball.
3. Your right hand may be too dominant. At the top of your backswing the left wrist should be in a strong position under the shaft.
4. The last three fingers of your left hand must hold the club firmly at the top of the backswing.
5. Slicing is often caused by placing the ball opposite your right foot. Address the ball between the inside of your left heel and the middle of the stance.
6. Hands and arms may be initiating the downswing. Start your hip action before moving any other part of your body.

Incorrect grip which produces slice. The V formed by the thumb and index finger of the right hand points straight up. The left hand grip has moved too far to the left.

Error: Hooking

Result: The clubhead contacts the ball with a closed face which projects your ball on a curved flight to the left.

The line shows the correct position of the clubface.

The V's formed by the thumbs and index fingers point too far to the right.

Correction:
1. Examine your grip.
   a. Your left hand may be too far to the right. Put the thumb of your left hand just to the right of the center of the shaft.
   b. Your right hand may have slipped too far under the shaft. Readjust your grip to place the thumb of the right hand slightly to the left of the center of the shaft.
2. Your backswing may be flat. This is a result of rolling your wrists to the right on your backswing and to the left on your downswing. Keep your wrists firm to avoid turning the shaft.
3. Your right hand may be lifting the clubhead as you start the backswing. Work on developing the one piece backswing.
4. In the address position, your right hand grip may be too strong. Develop a firm yet controlled left hand grip.
5. Your left arm may be collapsing during the swing. Concentrate on keeping your left arm extended throughout the total action.

Error: Pushing

Result: The flight of your ball is straight to the right of the intended target, caused by hitting from the outside in, with the clubface slightly open.
Correction:
1. The ball may be opposite your right heel. Play the ball according to your club, opposite the area between the center of your feet and your left heel.
2. Your body sway is too great. A sway too far to the right on the backswing encourages a sway too far to the left on the downswing.
3. Hands alone may be starting the swing. Start the clubhead back on the proper line with a unified action.
4. On the backswing the wrists may turn in such a way as to place the palm of the right hand under the club and the left palm on top. If your clubhead is square at the top of your backswing, your wrist position will be correct.
5. You may be lifting your head on the downswing. Keep your eyes over the ball and maintain a steady head position.

Error: Pulling

Result: The ball flies on a straight line to the left of the intended target caused by swinging the club too far outside the desired arc and ending too far inside.

"Incorrect"

"Correct"

Reaching for the ball at address produces a low flat backswing and closed clubface at impact.

Correction:
1. Grip may be too loose at the top of your backswing. Practice strengthening your left hand grip and maintain firm control of the club with the last three fingers of the left hand.
2. Clubhead may be out of the correct plane on your backswing. Start the backswing as a single unit, keeping the club on the inside.
3. Left shoulder should rotate under your chin; however, avoid forcibly dropping the shoulder too low. Concentrate on rotating your shoulder.
4. Hands and arms may be striking at the ball from the top of your backswing. Delay the unlocking of your wrists until your hands have traveled past waist level on your downswing.
5. Arms and hands may be leading on the downswing. Initiate the downswing by turning your hips.

Error: Topped ball
Result: The clubhead contacts your ball above the center line, sending the ball on a low flight or rolling across the ground.
Correction:
1. Avoid looking up before your ball has left the ground. When you lift the head, the shoulders and club follow. Establish a smooth rhythmical swing with no lifting of your shoulders or jerking of your head. Keep the head down until you are well into the follow-through.
2. You may be lifting your shoulders as a result of tension. Work on developing a smooth rhythmical swing.
3. Check to see if you have too much weight on the left foot at the top of your backswing. When this occurs, your weight is shifted improperly to your right foot on the downswing and you chip the ball. At the top of the backswing your weight should be toward the inside of the right foot.
4. You may be lifting the club with your hands as you start the backswing. Keep the clubhead in contact with grass as long as possible on your backswing and concentrate on a unified movement of the arms, hands, hips and shoulders.
5. In the address position check your distance from the ball. If the ball is too close, you may subconsciously raise your body to avoid hitting the ground. When the ball is too far away, you will not be able to get the club squarely behind it.
6. A sway to your right on the backswing, that is not followed by a sway to the left in your downswing, leaves your body too far to the right. Keep your body sway to a minimum.

Isolated Movements of the Swing

Takeaway

The backswing or takeaway is a simultaneous movement of the hips, arms and shoulders. To gain a longer arc on your swing, keep your clubhead low as long as possible. Practice the takeaway as a recoiling action of your forward press.

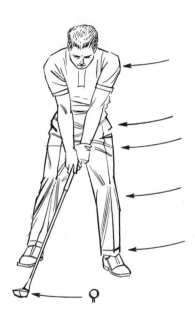

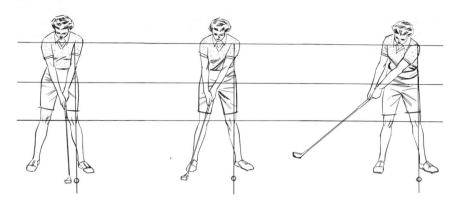

Knee action

The knee action starts with a forward press with your right knee.

Your weight is on the instep of the right foot. Left knee is pointing just behind the ball. Left heel may be raised.

"Correct"   "Incorrect"

Transfer your weight from the right foot toward the left leg.

Follow-through until the weight has completely transferred to the left foot; right heel is off the ground.

The right arm

At address, the right elbow is close to your body; the right palm is facing your target.

At the top, the right arm is flexed with the elbow pointing toward the ground. The right arm will move slightly away from your body.

On downswing, the right elbow returns close to the body. Inside of your right arm faces outward.

At impact, right arm is more extended with the palm of your right hand facing the target.

Wrist action

Start your downswing with your wrists cocked and the left arm pulling the end of the club toward the ground.

Delay the uncocking action of your wrists until your hands reach hip level. Late uncocking of the wrists will give you an acceleration of the right hand action.

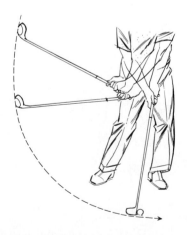

To prevent uncocking your wrists too early, concentrate on keeping your hands ahead of the clubhead as long as possible.

Practice Hints for the Swing

1. Many people have difficulty in taking the clubhead back without turning the shaft and keeping a square position of the face of the club at impact. To correct this, take a square stance and address the ball, but do not use a club. With your hands open, approximate their normal position on the club. The back of the left hand and the palm of the right hand will be in a square position to the target.

Practice moving the right hand through the swinging motion, concentrating on keeping the hand square to the target as long as possible. Repeat with the left hand, and then place both hands close together and repeat the swinging motion.

2. To practice your arm position at address, address the ball and have a partner place a club under your left arm and over your right arm. The club should be in a straight line since your right arm at address is slightly lower than your left arm.

3. If you have trouble keeping your head steady, take the address position and have a partner place his hand on top of your head. Execute a full swing and notice whether your head stays on his hand or moves away from it.

Test to determine sway of head

4. There may be a tendency to strike the ball with your right arm. Take your right hand off the club and practice swinging with your left arm. After you have gained control of the club with your left hand, place the right hand on the club and continue swinging. The right arm should be passive.

The instructor or a partner can assist you by placing his left hand on your club. Finish the grip by placing your right hand on his left hand. In this position as he swings the club through a short swing, you should be able to feel his left arm controlling the swing and your right arm following. Perform the same action with your left hand and his right hand on the club.

5. A technique similar to the above will be helpful when you are swinging the club too far on the outside or too far on the inside of your target line. Take your grip with both hands on the club. The instructor or partner stands to the side and behind you and moves your club through the correct line, repeatedly, until you develop a feeling of the correct movement.

6. To determine whether you are swinging your club to the inside or to the outside of your target line, place a tee in the ground a few inches in front of your ball and along the path your club will

Tee Test—Line shows correct swing that would remove tee

follow. If your swing is correct the clubhead should contact the tee on your follow-through. When you wish to locate the exact line your clubhead travels on the follow-through, place several tees parallel to and in front of the ball. As the clubhead travels forward, a path will be cleared through the tees.

Other Approach Shots

When you are considering an approach to the green, evaluate: (1) the lie of the ball, (2) the amount of green between your ball and the hole, (3) the overall distance from the hole, (4) the contour of the green and (5) the ability you have with each club. Establish a definite plan of action based on your conclusion. Select a spot on the green where your ball should land. When the green is not wet or sloped, aim toward a spot approximately two club lengths in front of the green. Use the least lofted club that will place the ball on your target. For a downhill shot or for an approach to a fast green, select a club with more loft. The type of approach shot you make may be a chip shot, a pitch, or a pitch and run. They are much alike. Since you have already learned the techniques of making the chip shot, the pitch and the pitch and run will be presented in the form of a checklist.

Pitch

CHECKLIST
1. Used when the cup is close to the edge of the green or when there is a hazard between you and the hole.
2. Select a 9 iron or a pitching wedge.
3. Grip down on the shaft of your club.
4. Play from an open stance with your feet close together and your weight on the left foot.
5. Weight does not shift.
6. Place the ball slightly in the direction of your right foot.
7. Swing is restricted to your hands and your arms.
8. Cock your wrist while lifting the clubhead—use hand and wrist action to hit the ball with a descending blow.
9. Rely on the loft of the club to get the ball into the air.
10. Club should contact the ball first, before hitting the ground.

Pitch, No. 9 iron or pitching wedge

Pitch and run

1. Strive for lower flight of ball with more roll.
2. Use a less lofted club that will land the ball on your target and roll the ball toward the hole.
3. Slightly open stance.
4. Aim short of the green to allow for roll.
5. Very little body and leg movement.
6. Essentially same swing as your chip shot except that there is more body action and a longer backswing.
7. Swing is a slow, smooth, effortless action.

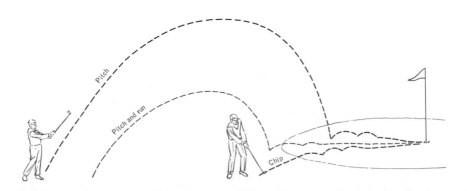

Use the No. 8 iron for a chip shot when the cup is close; a No. 5, 6 or 7 iron would run past the hole.

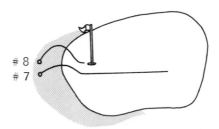

When there is trouble between you and the hole, and the pin is toward the back of the green, use a pitch and run shot that will give you a high loft and then will run to the hole.

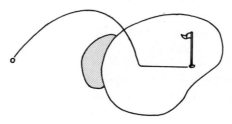

Use the No. 9 iron when you desire a high loft of the ball with little or no run.

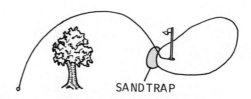

Trouble Shots

Hilly and rough terrain and sand traps are the chief offenders in creating difficult shots for the golfer. Playing the ball from uneven terrain, the grass of the rough or the sand presents special problems that must be solved with special techniques.

Uphill lie

An uphill lie of the ball occurs when the ball has come to rest on a hill slanting upward toward the target. The more uphill the lie, the higher and shorter the ball will fly.

HINTS FOR PLAYING AN UPHILL LIE

1. Similar to your normal fairway shot except the weight is slightly more on your right side.
2. Open stance.
3. Play the ball toward your higher foot.
4. Take the clubhead straight away from the ball, following the contour of the ground; hit down and swing through.
5. Ball tends to travel a little higher and thus not so far. Compensate by selecting a longer club.
6. Aim to the right of your target as the ball has a tendency to hook.

Downhill lie

A downhill lie is a condition in which the ball has come to rest on a hill that is slanting down toward the target.

Hints for playing a downhill lie:

1. Center of gravity is forward, therefore slightly bend your up-hill knee until your hips are level.
2. Open stance.
3. Play the ball to the left of the center of your stance.
4. Ball will travel lower and roll farther. Compensate by selecting one club less than you would for a normal shot.
5. Take-away is normal, but on the downswing let your club follow the contour of the ground as far as you can.
6. Aim to the left of your target as the ball has a tendency to slice.

When the ball is below your feet be-cause you are on the side of the hill, open your stance and transfer your weight toward your heels. Flex your knees more than usual and take a slow swing. There is a tendency to fade or push the ball to the right. Follow the contour of the hill on both the backswing and the follow-through.

Playing the ball below feet

If the ball is above your feet, choke down on the shaft of your club. Use your normal club for the same distance. Follow the slope of the hill on both the backswing and the follow-through. Since there is a tendency to hook or pull the shot, aim to the right of your target.

Playing the ball above feet

Playing out of Rough

In playing out of the rough the chief concern is getting back on the fairway in the best possible position to continue on to the target.

Selection of the club will depend upon your distance from the hole and the depth of the grass. For a short distance, use your wedge. The heavy flange of the wedge cuts through the grass and the extra loft lifts the ball rapidly. When you have a long distance to go and the rough is light or medium, use either a 3 or 4 wood. Play the ball opposite your left foot.

For heavy rough take your club with the highest loft, face the fairway and swing hard. You may find it advantageous to take a penalty stroke and drop the ball out of the rough as provided in the rules.

Light rough

Take a club with enough loft to lift the ball from the rough. Aim short of your target as the ball will have more roll.

Medium rough

Take your club with the highest loft and aim toward the fairway but also in the direction of the hole.

Heavy rough

Sand Shot

The sand trap seems to present a psychological hazard, rather than a physical one. Essentially three things can go wrong: you can miss the ball, hit it too hard or hit it too soft. The recent development of the sand wedge has enabled players to become more proficient in blasting out of sand. The wedge is a heavy short shafted club designed to slide through the sand and under the ball.

When hitting a wedge shot near the green, you should attempt to get the ball out of the sand and onto the green in one shot. For a long sand shot that requires more flight of the ball, contact the sand closer to the ball. The closer the club is to your ball as it enters the sand, the farther the ball will travel in the air. As you approach your ball, notice the condition of the sand. If the sand is soft and dry, your clubhead will slide through the sand and build up sand in front of the ball, necessitating a forceful stroke. However, if the sand is hard, a lighter stroke should be used, as the clubhead will have a tendency to bounce. Establish a firm footing in the sand by pressing down with your feet and wiggling them into place. Remember that it is against the rules to sole your club in the sand trap.

Check points for sand shot

1. Open your stance with the feet wider than normal for a shot of the same distance.
2. Flex your knees more than you do on a normal shot.
3. Clubhead should be slightly open.
4. Ball is played slightly back from your left heel.
5. Use arm and hand control with little movement of your body or knees.

6. Keep your swing low and rely on the build in loft of the club to lift ball.
7. Strike the sand one and a half to three inches behind the ball.
8. Concentrate on swinging your clubhead through the sand.
9. Keep your head position steady and your eyes on the ball.

PUTTING

Putting is undoubtedly one of the most controversial techniques in the game of golf. There are nearly as many styles of putting as there are players.

As well as skill, putting requires concentration, relaxation and confidence. The most successful competitors in golf are the players who are proficient in putting and in approaching the green. This is apparent when you realize that during an 18 hole round of golf, 36 strokes are allocated to putting. You can lose a stroke on the fairway and make it up on the green, but a lost stroke on the green is gone.

Although the single purpose of the putt is to roll the ball over the green and into the hole, there are excellent putters who use vastly different techniques. When you observe the amateur and professional golf matches on television, notice such players as Arnold Palmer, Jack Nicklaus, Kathy Whitworth and Mickey Wright who are successful, yet differ in their style of putting. Some golfers prefer to use a shoulder stroke while others benefit more from a wrist action or a combination of both. The weight may be distributed over the left foot, the right foot or over both feet. The ball can be played on a line ranging from the left foot to the right foot. Recommendations for a stance include the closed or square stance; however, the majority of the golfers favor the square stance. As you can see, the position of the body while putting is a highly personal and individual matter. Consequently, since the purpose of the putt is to get the ball into the hole, use the techniques which prove most successful for you.

Selection of a putter

There is no one putter, made of a certain kind of material or with a particular shaft or grip, that is regarded as the best putter. Select a putter that appeals to you, then test it on the putting green to see that it is well balanced. Select one that will allow you to stand comfortably over the ball with the club soled correctly and your eyes over the ball. A few of the available putters are shown in the illustration.

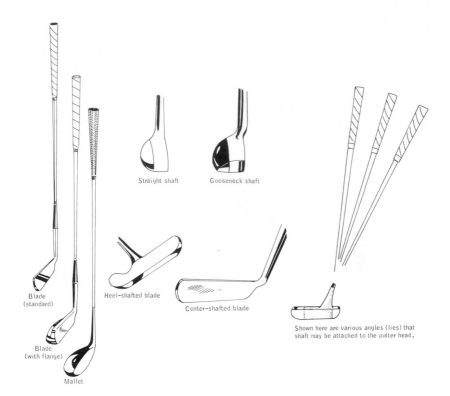

Straight shaft   Gooseneck shaft

Blade
(standard)   Heel-shafted blade

Center-shafted blade

Blade
(with flange)

Shown here are various angles (lies) that
shaft may be attached to the putter head.

Mallet

Condition of green

Before hitting the ball, all consistent putters evaluate the condition of the putting green. Consideration is given to the direction the grass is growing, the thickness of the grass, the slope of the green, the type of grass, and the moisture. The ball will have a tendency to roll faster on dry grass and slower on a wet surface. As you study the green, a shiny surface between you and the hole indicates you will be putting with the grain of the grass and the ball will roll faster. On the other hand, if the area between your ball and the hole seems dull or dark, you will be putting against the grain of the grass and will need to stroke the ball more firmly.

The Grip

The putting grip is another debatable issue. Golfers will frequently putt with the Vardon, the ten finger, the interlocking or the reverse overlap grip. Many players prefer to use the same grip they use with other clubs; however, you may wish to adopt the grip most commonly accepted, the reverse overlapping. As the name implies, the little finger of the right hand and the index finger of the left hand exchange places.

Analysis of the reverse overlapping grip

Place your right hand on the club with the palm in a square position toward the target line. Then put your left hand on the shaft with the index finger overlapping the right little finger. Your thumbs should be in a straight line down the center of the shaft. The left hand grip is a palm or finger grip while the right hand is a finger grip.

The index finger of your left hand overlaps right little finger.

Preparation techniques

Judgment of the putting distance and a feeling for contacting the ball with the correct amount of force are essential to good putting. More putts are missed by stroking too hard or too light than by stroking on the wrong line. To develop a feeling for stroking a putt smoothly into the cup, practice rolling the ball. Until you can consistently roll a ball into the cup, it will be difficult for you to hit the ball into the hole with an implement.

Before attempting to use a putter, stand about two feet in front of the hole, take a ball in your hand, lean over and roll the ball toward the cup. Use a gentle underarm motion and let the ball slowly roll off your fingertips. The ball may roll into the cup from the left side, the right side, the back or the front. Aim directly for the front of the cup; then, if the ball should go out of line in either direction, you still have a chance of sinking your putt.

After you are able to roll the ball into the cup from two feet, move back to four feet. You will notice that you must take a longer back-

swing and a longer follow-through. Continue moving back until you can successfully judge the various distances around the green. To co-ordinate this action with your putting, take a square stance, and hold the ball in your right hand with the palm square to the putting line. Lean over and gently roll the ball toward the cup. Repeat this from the various positions on the green. You should now possess a feeling for the gentleness and efficiency of the putting stroke.

Although the techniques suggested below are by no means the only ones you may use, they are the positions found most successful by a large percentage of players. It would be wise for you to experi-ment with putting techniques to develop the most proficient and the most comfortable position for you.

Analysis of putting stroke

Assume a square stance and place your feet close together. The ball should be opposite the large toe of your left foot. Stand with your eyes directly over the ball. The face of your putter should be square to the target.

Take the clubhead back in a low smooth motion. Keep the face of your club in a square position toward the target, using as little arm movement as possible.

As you stroke the ball, keep your arms close to your body. Hit the ball squarely but gently. The amount of backswing, and thus force, you will need at impact is determined by the distance of the putt and the condition of the green.

The face of your putter should be square to the putting line on the follow-through. You should feel as if the club is following the ball. Keep your head down until after you stroke the ball.

Putts that break

Stroke your downhill putts to travel slowly. If the ball is going fast, it may roll over the hole. The ball is susceptible to sidehill roll. Allow for more break (curvature of the ball) as you determine your aim.

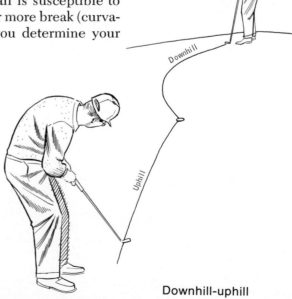

Downhill-uphill

Long putts

When you have a long putt, consider the position of your second putt to reach the hole. If you are putting uphill, play short to avoid going past the hole, as then you will be faced with the problems involved in stroking downhill.

Sidehill putts

When putting sidehill, your point of aim will be to the side of the hole. Putts are more susceptible to break when the speed of your ball is decreasing. Study the contour of the green around the hole.

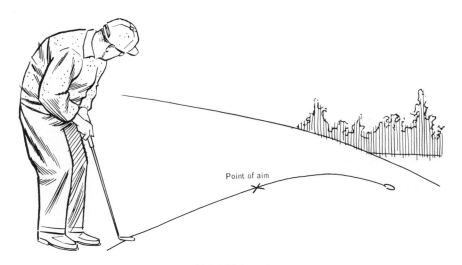

Point of aim

Sidehill break

Point of aim

Aim for the side of the cup for putts that will have a slight break. When the putt has a sharp break, your aim will be toward a spot along the intended line of the putt.

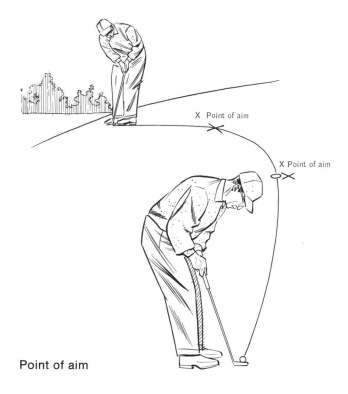

X Point of aim

X Point of aim

Point of aim

Errors and Correction

Error: Poor judgment of distance.

Result: The ball is short of the hole or rolls past the hole.

Correction: Go back to rolling the ball with your hand. Practice
this from varying distances. When you are able to roll the ball
successfully into the cup at each distance, then practice putting
the ball from each distance.

Error: No feeling for the putting stroke or inability to judge distance.

Result: Long putts do not reach the hole.

Correction: With a string, outline a circle three feet in diameter.
Putt toward the circle until you can hit four consecutive putts
inside the string. Change your position and repeat. As you become more proficient, make the circle smaller.

Error: Faulty stroke.

Result: The ball goes off the intended line of direction.

Correction: Practice studying the greens and align yourself correctly. The clubhead should be square at impact. The shaft should not be turned in the backswing or the follow-through. It may help to keep your eyes on a spot two inches to the left of the ball. The clubhead should be square as it passes this spot on your follow-through.

Practice Hints for Putting

1. To practice aligning the clubhead with the target, place two clubs on the green parallel to each other and in line with the target. Place the ball between the two clubs and practice your putting stroke inside of the area bounded by the two clubs.

2. When you are practicing your putting stroke on the green, place four balls two feet from the hole, one on each side of the hole. Practice hitting these balls into the cup. If you miss with any one of them, stop and start over. Continue until you are able to get all four balls into the hole. Repeat this same procedure placing the balls three, four, five and six feet from the hole.

3. Practice putting with your head and the head of your putter touching a wall. This will help you keep your head over the ball and the clubhead in a square position toward your target.

4

Rules

The official rules of golf in the United States of America for both men and women are established by the United States Golf Association. Few golfers realize that the United States Golf Association's rules are designed to protect as well as to penalize players. You can save many strokes by realizing your legal rights on the golf course and utilizing them. Since the approved rules are numerous and sometimes confusing to a beginning player, a summary of the basic rules and of the types of competition between individuals and among groups will be presented.

MATCH PLAY

A game is usually 18 holes or less in which you match your game hole by hole with your opponent. The side which has the least number of strokes on a hole wins that particular hole. When each side receives the same number of strokes on a hole, the hole is said to be halved (tied). Each side receives 1/2 point. The match is terminated when one side is leading by a number of holes greater than the number of holes remaining to be played or, in informal play, when you complete the total 18 holes.

HOLE	SCORER 1	2	3	4	5	6	7	8	9	OUT	10	11	12	13	14	15	16	17	18	IN	DATE TOTAL	HDCP	NET
PAR	5	3	4	4	5	4	4	4	3	36	4	4	3	4	4	3	4	4	5	35	71		
PLUS/MINUS																							
HANDICAP	7	17	9	1	11	3	13	5	15		8	14	18	10	2	16	4	12	6				
PAR FOR WOMEN	5	3	4	5	5	4	4	5	3	38	4	4	3	4	4	3	5	4	5	36	74		

Sample scoring 18 holes

Winner of hole	Score you–opponent		Match terminology
1–you	1	0	You–1 up; opp–1 down
2–you	2	0	You–2 up; opp–2 down
3–opp.	2	1	You–1 up; opp–1 down
4–opp.	2	2	Match even
5–halved	2½	2½	Match even
6–opp.	2½	3½	You–1 down; opp–1 up
7–you	3½	3½	Match even
8–you	4½	3½	You–1 up; opp–1 down
9–halved	5	4	You–1 up; opp–1 down
10–opp.	5	5	Match even
11–opp.	5	6	You–1 down; opp–1 up
12–you	6	6	Match even
13–halved	6½	6½	Match even
14–you	7½	6½	You–1 up; opp–1 down
15–opp.	7½	7½	Match even
16–opp.	7½	8½	You–1 down; opp–1 up
*17–opp.	7½	9½	You–2 down; opp–2 up
18–you	8½	9½	You–1 down; opp–1 up

*Match could have been terminated at the end of the seventeenth hole; since your opponent was leading by two holes (leading by more holes than the remaining number of holes left to play).

STROKE PLAY

You compare your total score for a round of golf, usually 18 holes, with your opponent's total score. The player with the least number of strokes for the round of golf wins.

Sample scoring

In the illustration, it took you a total of 83 shots to complete 18 holes of golf; your opponent needed 87. You would therefore win the match.

HOLE	1	2	3	4	5	6	7	8	9	OUT	10	11	12	13	14	15	16	17	18	IN	TOTAL	HDCP	NET
YOU	5	4	5	5	5	6	5	5	4	44	5	4	3	5	4	4	5	4	5	39	83		
OPPONENT	6	4	6	4	5	5	4	5	5	44	5	4	4	5	5	4	4	5	6	42	87		
PAR	5	3	4	4	5	4	4	4	3	36	4	4	3	4	4	3	4	4	5	35	71		
PLUS/MINUS																							
HANDICAP																							
PAR FOR WOMEN	5	3	4	5	5	4	4	5	3	38	4	4	3	4	4	3	5	4	5	36	74		

SCORER   DATE

RULES TO ASSIST YOU

1. *Casual water, ground under repair, hole made by burrowing animal* — Through the green you are entitled to take a free drop, no nearer the hole, but within two club lengths from the point on the outside edge of the hole nearest the original lie of the ball. If the ball is located in a hazard, you may drop the ball in the hazard; however, by accepting a one-stroke penalty you are entitled to drop the ball outside the trap. Since snow and ice are also considered casual water, the ball may be removed and dropped without penalty.

2. *Lost ball* — You are allowed five minutes to search for a lost ball. If your lost ball is in a water hazard, you are entitled to probe for the ball.

3. *Provisional ball* — You may play a provisional ball for a ball which you deem lost or out of bounds. The provisional ball must be played before you or your partner search for the original ball. If your opponent fails to notify you or your marker that he is hitting a provisional ball, the provisional ball becomes the ball in play and the original ball is abandoned. If you hit the original ball from the teeing ground, you may re-tee the provisional ball anywhere within the teeing area. On a fairway shot, you must drop the provisional ball near the spot from which the original ball was hit.

4. *Dropping ball* — When you drop the ball out of a hazard such as a ditch or a water hole, you are penalized one stroke; however, you are entitled to drop the ball anywhere, as long as you keep the spot at which the ball last crossed the hazard between you and the hole.

   (*a*) When a dropped ball stops in a position that continues to affect your stance or swing, there is no penalty, but you must re-drop the ball. Should this occur again, you must, without penalty, place the ball where it was last dropped.

   (*b*) If, in the process of dropping the ball, the ball touches you before touching the ground, you must re-drop the ball, with no penalty.

   (*c*) When a dropped ball strikes the ground and then touches you or rests against your feet and moves when you do, there is no penalty, but you play the ball where it comes to rest.

5. *Conceded putt* — When an opponent has conceded a putt to you, he is not allowed to retract his statement.

6. *Ball unplayable* — You are the sole judge of whether or not your ball is playable. Your ball may be determined unplayable at any place on the course with the exception of a water hazard. There is a one-stroke penalty; however, you are allowed to drop the ball within two clublengths of the point where it originally lay, but not nearer the hole, or you may drop the ball as far as you desire behind the point where the ball was hit. An unplayable lie in a bunker must be dropped in the trap.

7. *Ball hanging on lip* — When the ball of your opponent is on the edge of the cup, he is allowed only a few seconds to determine whether his ball is at rest. In match play, if he refuses to remove his ball and to allow play to continue, you have the right to concede a putt to him by removing his ball.

8. *Obstructions* — When your ball, stance or swing is blocked by a movable obstruction, you are permitted to remove the obstruction without penalty. Should your ball move in the process, you must replace it. When an immovable obstruction interferes with your ball, stance, or backswing you may drop the ball, without penalty, not more than two clublengths from the point on the outside of the obstruction nearest the original lie of the ball.

9. *Ball striking another on putting green* — In stroke play, if your opponent hits his ball in such a manner that it contacts your ball, he is penalized two strokes while you are permitted to replace your ball. In match play, if your opponent's ball strikes your ball, both of you may replace your balls without penalty; however, if his ball should knock your ball into the hole, you are considered to have holed out on your last stroke.

10. *Lifting ball* — When you have skulled or topped a ball, look to see if you put a cut on the cover. If there is no visible mark and you think there may be a cut on the bottom, you may, with no penalty, lift the ball in the presence of your opponent in match play or in the presence of the marker in stroke play.

11. *Out of bounds* — A ball is out of bounds when all of it lies out of bounds. You may therefore play any ball that does not lie completely out of bounds.

RULES FOR THE TEEING AREA

1. *Number of clubs* — You are entitled to carry a maximum of fourteen United States Golf Association approved golf clubs. Once selected, you must play with these clubs with the exception that you may replace any club that becomes unfit. If you commenced play with less than fourteen clubs, you are allowed to add to your number to make a total of fourteen.

Penalty

Match play — Two strokes for each hole in which the violation occurred.

Stroke play — Two strokes for each hole in which the violation occurred.

2. *Driving outside teeing ground*—When beginning play on a hole, you must hit your first ball from the teeing ground, a rectangular area two-clublengths in depth, from the front and side tee markers.

Penalty
> Match play—No penalty, but you must hit another ball from within the teeing area.
> Stroke play—You must count any stroke illegally played and then hit another shot from the proper teeing area.

3. *Ball falling off tee*—A ball that falls off or is accidentally knocked off the tee during your address may be replaced.

No penalty

4. *Honor*—On the first tee, you determine by lot or draw who is to have the honor of hitting first; thereafter, the honor is awarded to the winner of the previous hole. When a hole is halved, the player who had the honor on the previous hole retains it.

Penalty
> Match play—No penalty, but the ball must be replayed from the tee in the proper order.
> Stroke play—No penalty and the ball remains in play.

5. *Order of play*—When playing in a threesome or foursome, you and your partner must hit the ball alternately from the teeing ground of each hole.

Penalty
> Match play—No penalty, but your opponent may request that you replay your ball from the teeing ground in the proper order.
> Stroke play—No penalty and your ball is considered in play.

RULES FOR THE FAIRWAY

1. *Cleaning ball*—You are permitted to lift your ball and in the process clean it when retrieving a ball from an unplayable lie, an obstruction, a water hazard, ground under repair or casual water. You are otherwise restricted from cleaning your ball on the fairway, except when it is necessary for identification.

Penalty
> Match play—Loss of hole.
> Stroke play—Two strokes.

2. *Ball moving at address* — When addressing your ball on the fairway, you may touch the ball with your clubhead, provided the ball does not move.

Penalty
   Match play — Penalty stroke.
   Stroke play — Penalty stroke.

3. *Ball unfit* — You may consider your ball to be unfit for play; however, you must make the substitution on the hole in which the damage occurred and in the presence of an opponent or the marker, in stroke play.

Penalty
   Match play — Loss of hole.
   Stroke play — Two strokes.

4. *Obstruction* — If your ball lands in or touches casual water, ground under repair or a hole caused by some animal or bird, you are permitted to lift the ball and drop it on the ground free of interference. You must, however, drop the ball within two club lengths from the point on the outside edge of the obstruction that is nearest the original lie of the ball.

Penalty
   None.

5. *Obstruction within a hazard* — When your ball lands in a hazard and touches casual water, ground under repair or a hole, you may lift your ball and drop it on the ground in the hazard which is free of the interference. The drop must be made as close as possible to the original lie of the ball, but not nearer the hole.

Penalty
   Match play — No penalty.
   Stroke play — No penalty.

If you agree to accept a one-stroke penalty, you may drop the ball outside of the hazard. You must keep the original lie of the ball between you and the hole and avoid dropping the ball nearer the hole.

6. *Lost ball* — When you lose your ball in casual water, ground under repair or a hole made by an animal, you are allowed to drop a ball as near as possible to the spot where the ball last crossed the hazard, but not closer to the hole.

Penalty
   None.

7. *Soling club in hazard*—While addressing a ball in a sand trap or in a water hazard, you must avoid touching the sand or the water with your clubhead.

Penalty
 Match play—Loss of hole.
 Stroke play—Two strokes.

8. *Lost ball in water hazard*—If your ball is at rest or is lost in a water hazard, you may drop the ball anywhere behind the hazard, as long as you keep the spot at which the ball crossed the margin of the hazard between you and the hole.

Penalty
 Match play—Penalty stroke.
 Stroke play—Penalty stroke.

9. *Dropping ball*—When you are entitled to drop the ball, select the proper distance, stand erect, face the hole and drop the ball behind you over your shoulder.

Penalty
 Match play—One stroke.
 Stroke play—One stroke.

10. *Advice*—While on the golf course, you are allowed to give or to receive advice only from your caddy, your partner and your partner's caddy.

Penalty
 Match play—Loss of hole.
 Stroke play—Two strokes.

11. *Loose impediment*—It is permissible to remove any loose objects such as stones, twigs and leaves which interfere with your stance, stroke or ball. An exception to this rule exists if both the ball and the loose impediment are in or touch a hazard.

Penalty
 Match play—Loss of hole.
 Stroke play—Two strokes.

RULES FOR THE PUTTING GREEN

1. *Unattended flagstick*—When your approach shot lands against an unattended flagstick, you are entitled to remove the flagstick. If

your ball subsequently rolls into the hole, you are deemed to have
holed out.

Penalty
  Match play — None.
  Stroke play — None.

When you play the ball from the putting green, you should avoid
hitting an unattended flagstick.

Penalty
  Match play — Loss of hole.
  Stroke play — Two strokes.

2. *Cleaning ball* — You are entitled to lift your ball and clean it
only before your first putt.

Penalty
  Match play — One stroke.
  Stroke play — One stroke.

3. *Touching putting line* — While putting, you may not make a
stroke on the putting green from a stance astride the putting line, with
either foot touching the putting line, or with either foot touching an
extension of that line. The putting line is not necessarily a straight
line, but the intended line of travel to the hole.

Penalty
  Match play — Loss of hole.
  Stroke play — Two strokes.

4. *Continuous putting* — Beginning with the player who is farthest away, you must putt continuously until you have holed out. An
exception to this rule exists when continuous putting would force
you to stand on a competitor's line of play.

Penalty
  Match play — One stroke.
  Stroke play — One stroke.

5. *Interference on green* — Should your ball land in casual water,
ground under repair or a hole made by an animal or if these conditions
exist between your ball and the hole, you may lift the ball and place
it in a position which offers relief from the interference. The place-
ment must be made as near the original lie as possible but not nearer
the hole.

Penalty
  Match play — No penalty.
  Stroke play — No penalty.

6. *Attended flagstick* — If the flagstick is attended, your ball may not contact the flagstick, the person attending it or the equipment he carries.

Penalty
  Match play — Loss of hole.
  Stroke play — Two strokes.

INDIVIDUAL AND GROUP GOLF COMPETITIONS

There are a variety of games and matches devised for competition in golf extending from formal United States Golf Association sponsored golf tournaments to novelty tournaments conducted by local clubs or organizations. Each sponsoring group has its favorite type of matches; however, the examples listed below are the most common.

Best Ball (Four Ball-Low Ball)

Best ball competition, often referred to as four ball, consists of hole by hole competition in which you and a partner play against two opponents. On hole No. 1 each one of you plays a ball as you normally do, then you match the lower score made by you and your teammate against the lower score obtained by your opponents. A single point is awarded to the side that has the lower score. If the low score of your team is the same as your opponents', the hole is considered tied and no point is awarded to either team. You then progress to hole No. 2 where you continue in the same manner until you have completed your specific round of golf.

Best Ball					
	Team A		*Team B*		
Hole	You	Partner	Opponents		Hole Score	Match Score
1	6	5	7	6	Won by Team A	1-Up Team A
2	6	7	7	6	Even	1-Up Team A
					1-Up Team A	

Since the score of 5 made by your partner on hole No. 1 is lower than the seven and six recorded by your opponents, your team is awarded one point. Your team is said to be 1-up. On hole No. 2, your low score of 6 is the same as the six shot by an opponent, thus no point is awarded and the match score remains 1-up.

Low Ball—Low Total

Another type of foursome competition is low ball-low total in which two points are awarded for each hole. One point for the team with the lower individual score (as in best ball) and one point for the team with the lower total score. You and your partner will match your best score for each hole and your total score for each hole against the best score and the total score of your opponents. The team with the lower individual score wins a point and the team with the lower total score wins a point. If you tie an opponent for low ball or low total, no point is given.

Low Ball—Low Total						
	Team A		Team B			
Hole	You	Teammate	Opponents		Hole Score	Match Score
1	5	4	6	7	2 points	Team A 1-up
2	5	8	6	6	Even	
						Team A 1-up

On hole No. 1 your teammate scored a 4 which is lower than the 6 or 7 scored by your opponents. The total score for your team is 9 and, therefore, lower than the total score of 13 shot by your opponents. Your team is awarded 2 points and the match score is 1-up in your favor.

On hole number two, your five takes low ball; however, your opponents' total score of 12 is lower than your team score of 13. A point is awarded to each team, resulting in a tie score for the hole. The hole score is considered even, on hole number 2, with your match score remaining 1-up.

Nassau

The Nassau system is a flexible type of golf match that is either match or stroke play and may be for a twosome, a threesome or a foursome. Three points are awarded—one for the winner of the first nine, one point for the second nine and one point for the total eighteen holes. When three of you are participating in stroke play, it is possible for each of you to win one point or for one person to win all of the points.

Stroke Play			
	You	*Player A*	*Player B*
Score 1st 9	42	38	39	1 point to Player A
Score 2nd 9	42	45	43	1 point to you
Score 18 holes	84	83	82	1 point to Player B

Three Ball

If you are playing in a threesome, you may wish to compete in a three ball match. Three ball is a type of stroke play or match play competition in which you and two opponents are playing against each other. In stroke play you weight your low total score against the low score of each opponent, whereas in match play you compete hole-by-hole against each opponent.

Scotch Foursome

As the name "Scotch" implies, this is a match in which you and your partner use one ball to compete against two opponents who alternately hit one ball.

To begin the match each contestant hits a tee shot; however, instead of playing all four balls each team selects its best ball. All subsequent shots are hit alternately until you have completed the hole. Let us assume that your partner hits a better tee shot than you; you would pick up your ball and would hit your partner's ball. This would be counted as the second stroke for your team.

THE HANDICAP

To understand the various handicapping systems you must become familiar with certain terms and definitions. Most often, the handicap is used "to provide fair and close competition between two players of unequal ability." As an individual player, you are able to "assess your over-all playing ability by determining the difference between your average game and par for the course."

Gross score and net score are frequently used in competition and in calculating handicaps. Gross score is the total number of strokes you took during an eighteen hole round. Net score is your gross score minus your handicap. Assuming that you have a gross score of 100 and a handicap of 20, your net score is 80.

Originally handicaps were established in relation to the best player of the local club. His score was automatically considered scratch or par and the other players were then ranked accordingly. Not too many players on a local course are able to play scratch golf, and a scratch player of one club cannot be compared to scratch players on all courses. Other clubs adjusted handicaps in relation to a par figure so liberally calculated that the most skillful players were given extra points.

The first universally accepted system of handicapping is attributed to the efforts of the British Ladies' Golf Union, an amateur organization formed in 1893. Over a period of years, the Ladies' Golf Union modified its method of handicapping until it proved reasonably accurate from club to club.

Any handicap system must naturally take into consideration the difficulty and the length of a hole. Since golf courses vary as much as a thousand yards in distance, a player cannot expect to obtain the same score on a 5,000 yard course as on a 4,000 yard course.

Since handicaps reflect your current playing ability, they should be periodically revised. If you are a regular playing member of a local club, the golf professional will keep a record of your scores and readjust your handicap (usually monthly). The United States Golf Association's recommendation is to base your handicap on the best 10 scores of the last 20 rounds of golf you have played.

Gentlemen's Agreement

Golfers frequently apply the handicap in match play. A designated number of strokes per hole (usually one-half to three) is awarded to the weaker player. This is more in terms of a gentlemen's agreement between you and your opponent. If there is a 14 stroke difference between your handicap and the handicap of your opponent, you may give him a stroke on all par four and par five holes. Strokes are seldom granted on par three holes, except when your opponent has a handicap of eighteen or more.

HOLE	1	2	3	4	5	6	7	8	9	OUT	10	11	12	13	14	15	16	17	18	IN	TOTAL	HDCP	NET
SCORER																	DATE						
PAR	5	3	4	4	5	4	4	4	3	36	4	4	3	4	4	3	4	4	5	35	71		
PLUS/MINUS																							
HANDICAP	7	17	9	1	11	3	13	5	15		8	14	18	10	2	16	4	12	6				
PAR FOR WOMEN	5	3	4	5	5	4	4	5	3	38	4	4	3	4	4	3	5	4	5	36	74		

Match Play With Handicap

Even though you are entitled to a handicap, the club often ranks the difficulty of each hole and designates the holes on which you may receive the strokes. Let's assume you have a handicap of six and your opponent has a handicap of three. You will, therefore, receive a three stroke handicap. The holes on which you are permitted to take your strokes are assigned in the handicap column on most score cards. The 18 holes of the course are ranked from one to eighteen, with the most difficult hole considered as handicap hole number one, the next most difficult as number two, etc. As shown by the illustration, you would deduct a stroke for holes 4, 14 and 6.

Stroke Play With Handicap

Assuming you have a handicap of 10 and your opponent has a 15 stroke handicap, you would grant him five strokes. If you score 83 on the 18 holes and your opponent scores 87, he would be the winner by one stroke.

	You	Opponent	
Handicap	10	15	= 5 strokes to opponent
Score 18 holes	83	87	
		–5	(his five stroke handicap)
	—	—	
Final Handicap Score	83	82	

SCORER DATE

HOLE	1	2	3	4	5	6	7	8	9	OUT	10	11	12	13	14	15	16	17	18	IN	TOTAL	HDCP	NET
YOU	5	4	5	5	5	6	5	5	4	44	5	4	3	5	4	4	5	4	5	39	83		83
OPPONENT	6	4	6	4	5	5	4	5	5	44	5	4	4	5	5	4	5	5	6	43	87	5	82
PAR	5	3	4	4	5	4	4	4	3	36	4	4	3	4	4	3	4	4	5	35	71		
PLUS/MINUS																							
HANDICAP	7	17	9	1	11	3	13	5	15		8	14	18	10	2	16	4	12	6				
PAR FOR WOMEN	5	3	4	5	5	4	4	5	3	38	4	4	3	4	4	3	5	4	5	36	74		

Simplified Handicap

A simplified handicap is "based on the scores for your last five games and on the par for the golf courses." To compute your simplified handicap, follow these five steps:

1. Add your last 5 games.
2. Add the par of the 5 courses over which you played your last 5 games.
3. Subtract the total of the pars from the total of your games.
4. Divide the difference by 5.
5. Divide the number obtained in step 4 by 7/8.

Simplified Handicap

Step 1	Step 2	Step 3	Step 4	Step 5
80	72	397		
75	73	363		
82	72	—		
84	72	34	$34 \div 5 = 6.8$	$6.8 \div 7/8 = 7.7$ or 8
76	74			stroke handicap
—	—			
397	363			

Callaway System

The Callaway system of automatic handicapping, developed in recent years, protects those who want to participate in a golfing event but who have no formal handicap. With this system, the handicap is based on the gross score for a single round of golf and on the highest scores for individual holes. Let us assume that your gross score for 18 holes of golf is 100. Find 100 on the Callaway Computation Chart. The 100 indicates that you are allowed to subtract, as your handicap, the total of your worst three holes. If your highest scores were an eight on hole 16, a nine on hole 12 and a ten on hole 4, you would deduct 27 from your total of 100 which would give you a net score of 73.

Callaway Chart - Computation Chart

CLASS A

Gross Score	Deduct
Par or less	Scratch
One over par to 75	1/2 worst hole
76 to 80	Worst hole
81 to 85	Worst hole plus 1/2 next
86 to 90	Two worst holes
91 to 95	Two worst holes plus 1/2 next
96 to 100	Three worst holes

CLASS B

101 to 105	Three worst holes plus 1/2 next
106 to 110	Four worst holes
111 to 115	Four worst holes plus 1/2 next
116 to 120	Five worst holes
121 to 125	Five worst holes plus 1/2 next

CLASS C

126 to 130	Six worst holes
131 to 135	Six worst holes plus 1/2 next
136 to 140	Seven worst holes
141 to 145	Seven worst holes plus 1/2 next
146 to 150	Eight worst holes

Novelty Competition

Beat the Pro—Each club member attempts to beat the gross score obtained by the club professional. As a club member, you are allowed to match your net score against the score of the professional.

Blind Bogey—Stroke play competition against an unannounced score. Before hitting a tee shot estimate the handicap you will need to have a net score between 70-80. As soon as the last contestant has finished his tee shot, a committee arbitrarily selects a "blind" number between 70 and 80. This score remains a secret until all players have finished 18 holes and turned in their score cards. The winner is the person whose net score is the closest to the blind bogey score.

Blind-Hole-Match—Competition in which you utilize your full handicap while playing 18 holes. As soon as you have completed your first tee shot, a committee will select nine blind holes. The scores you make on these holes are totaled to determine the winner.

Foursome Best Ball—A type of stroke play competition between teams of four people. Every member of your team hits a tee shot, then you decide whose ball is in the best position. If your ball is in the best position, all your team members will hit a second shot from that position. Play continues in the same manner until everyone has holed out. The lowest score of your team is recorded.

Throw-out—A type of stroke play competition in which you are entitled to subtract the scores of your three highest holes from your 18 hole total. The winner is the person who obtains the lowest score for 15 holes.

TOURNAMENTS

Medal tournament

Tournaments may be scheduled for one day (18 holes), two days (36 holes), three days (54 holes) or four days (72 holes). Although there is no minimum or maximum number of holes necessary for a medal tournament, it is usually an 18, 36 or 54 hole event. If you are participating in a 54 hole tournament, your original starting time is determined by your qualifying score or by lot. On the following two days, your starting time is assigned according to your score for the preceding round or rounds. Players with the highest scores tee off first, whereas contestants with the lowest scores are placed last.

Match tournament

A match play tournament is a type of elimination tournament in which you engage in hole by hole competition against designated opponents. Those who qualify are grouped into flights according to qualifying scores. Flights are listed as:

Championship—the top flight, therefore, includes the best players.

Flight A (or President's flight).

Flight B.

Flight C, and so forth.

Each then competes within the assigned flight. One will be the victor of each flight; however, the winner of the tournament is the person who wins the championship flight. Other flight champions are listed as: Miss Brown, winner of Flight A, Mrs. Smith, winner of Flight B, and so forth.

U.S. Golf Association Tournaments

Throughout the year there are innumerable amateur and professional golf tournaments conducted for participants of all ages and both sexes in the United States. Since it would be impossible to discuss each of the golf tournaments, only those sponsored by the United States Golf Association will be presented. As well as establishing the rules of golf, the United States Golf Association determines what constitutes amateur and professional status of golfers, maintains a handicapping system, and annually sponsors nine national competitions and five international events. The inauguration of the United States Golf Association sponsored tournaments occurred in 1895 when the organization conducted the United States Men's Amateur Championship. With the addition of the Senior Women's Amateur Championship in 1962, every man, woman and child in the United States of America who is a member of a United States Golf Association Regular Member Club is eligible to participate in a United States Golf Association sponsored championship.

Men's Amateur Championship

The Men's Amateur is a 72 hole stroke play tournament open to amateur golfers with handicaps of three strokes or less. Through a 36 hole sectional qualifying round, 150 players are selected for the championship play-off. All contestants compete in two 18 hole rounds of golf. The 60 players who obtain the lowest scores qualify for two additional rounds. The golfer with the lowest score for 72 holes becomes the men's amateur champion.

Open Championship

This tournament is a 72 hole stroke play competition open to both professional and amateur golfers who possess handicaps of two strokes or less. Through 36 hole local and 36 hole sectional qualifying rounds, 150 players are selected for the championship play-off. Following 36 holes of stroke play competition, each participant competes in an 18 hole round of golf. The fifty players with the lowest scores are selected to play in the final two 18 hole rounds. The champion is the person who has the lowest score for the 72 holes.

Amateur Public Links

This is a match play tournament open to amateur golfers who have been public course players since January 1 of the current year. Although the tournament is match play, there is a 36 hole stroke play qualifying round. The 64 players who qualify with the lowest scores engage in six rounds of match play.

Junior Amateur Championship

This is a combination stroke and match play tournament open to boys under 18 years of age who have handicaps of 10 strokes or less (no golf club membership is required). The 150 contestants are selected through 18 hole sectional qualifying rounds. Participants then engage in two 18 hole rounds of stroke play competition. The 64 amateurs with the lowest scores for the 36 holes are eligible for match play.

Senior Amateur

The Senior Amateur is a match play tournament open to men 55 years of age or older, who possess United States Golf Association handicaps of 10 strokes or less. A 36 hole stroke play qualifying round precedes the tournament. The 32 players who obtain the lowest scores qualify for the five rounds of match play competition.

Walker Cup Match

The match consists of a series of biennial team competitions between amateur male golfers of the United States and the British Isles. The United States team consists of 10 players and a captain selected by the United States Golf Association. The British Isles team is composed of 10 players and a captain selected from England, Scotland, Wales, Northern Ireland and Eire.

America's Golf Cup Match

In this contest a series of matches is held biennially between teams of amateur male golfers from golf clubs under the jurisdiction of the United States Golf Association, the Royal Canadian Golf Association, and the Association Mexicana de Golf. Teams consist of not more than seven players and a captain.

World Amateur Team Championship

This 72 hole stroke play amateur tournament is sponsored by the World Amateur Golf Council, and is open to leading amateurs of 46 countries. The tournament is rotated among the geographical zones of Europe, Africa, America, and Australia.

Tournaments for Women

Amateur Championships

This is a match play tournament open to women amateur golfers who possess handicaps of five strokes or less. Entries which include foreign competitors are limited to 150 players. Following a 36 hole stroke play qualifying round, the 32 players with the lowest scores are selected for the championship flight.

Girls' Junior Championship

This annual match play tournament is open to 140 girl amateur golfers who are less than 18 years of age and who possess handicaps of not more than 20 strokes. The 140 positions in the qualifying round are offered to the applicants with the lowest handicaps. The 32 positions available in the championship flight are selected through a 36 hole qualifying round.

Women's Open Championship

The Women's Open is a 72 hole stroke play competion open to both amateur and professional golfers with handicaps of five strokes or less. All contestants participate in the first two 18 hole rounds of play. The 40 women who obtain the lowest scores are eligible for the final 36 holes.

Senior Women's Amateur

This is a 54 hole medal play tournament planned specifically for women 55 years of age or over who have handicaps of 15 strokes or less. Entries are limited to 120 players with the 32 contestants in the championship flight selected through an 18 hole qualifying round.

Curtis Cup Matches

The Curtis Cup Matches are a biennial series of matches, held alternately in the United States and in the British Isles, between the leading women amateurs of the United States and the British Isles. Teams consist of eight players and a captain for each side. The United States Golf Association selects the leading amateur golfers of the United States while the Ladies Golf Union selects the players for the British team from the leading amateurs of England, Scotland, Wales, Northern Ireland, and Eire.

5

Strategy

It is impractical to take you through an imaginary 18 hole round of golf, for no two courses are constructed exactly the same. They all, however, include such similar, architecturally conceived hazards as dog legs (bends or curves in the fairway), bunkers, narrow greens, tall rough, trees and water. Attention should be placed on the application of your knowledge in relation to these man-made hazards.

More often than not, the champion is not the person who is able to make the best shots but is, instead, the player who is able to play the round with the least number of mistakes. A person with a good swing but no strategy on the course is referred to as "a good hitter but a bad player." While in the process of learning to play, forget about your score and concentrate on developing a consistent swing. Once you have accomplished the grip, the stance and the swing, the next step is the application of your knowledge.

GENERAL

Your best golf is played when you have established the proper mental attitude and frame of mind. First of all, leave your family and school problems in the locker room. Arrive at the course early enough to spend some time on the practice range. No professional golfer ever plays without warming up, yet an average golfer seldom spends any time on the practice tee. Have you ever wondered why so many weekend golfers play the second nine better than the first? The front nine has been their practice round!

Develop confidence in your ability to select the proper club. A major consideration is the distance from the hole, but you should also consider such items as the lie of the ball, the wind, the area to which you are hitting, the slope of the area and the hazards in your line of play. Confidence in your choice of club is heightened by: (1)

knowledge of your distance with each club and (2) knowledge of your ability to accurately determine your distance from the hole. While all golfers will take a chance every now and then, the skillful players learn when to gamble and when to play it safe. Tommy Armour, considered the master of the irons, developed the following two rules for lowering the score:

1. Play the shot you have the greatest chance of playing well.
2. Play the shot that makes the next shot easy.

After you have become more skilled, you will be able to take more chances with less risk of a catastrophe.

Be cautious of letting down mentally after playing a good hole or several good holes. The tendency is to relax and to let up on your concentration. Keep your mind on the task at hand, which is to get the ball in the hole with the least number of strokes.

Familiarize yourself with the course you are playing. If possible, walk over it and make sketches of the distance and the dangers of each hole. Place your shot in a position to take advantage of any slope in the fairway. Remember a ball will roll in the direction of the slope.

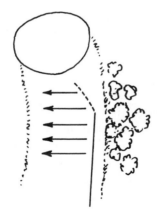

In the above illustration a ball hit to the right side of the green will roll to the middle of the fairway. Should your ball land in the trees or on the rough on the right side, it still has a chance to roll onto the fairway.

Establish a routine for each shot and do not try to change the system for different clubs. You will rapidly find that as soon as you start your routine, you are able to concentrate and keep your mind on hitting the ball. A simple method is to:

1. Analyze the lie of the ball on your way to it.
2. Select your club.
3. Find your target.
4. Grip the club correctly.
5. Take your stance.
6. Swing.

TEE SHOTS

The most advantageous position for teeing your ball is determined by the condition of the teeing surface and the location of your target. For example, if your target is on the left side of the fairway, tee the ball on the left side of the teeing ground. An exception to this will occur when the slope at the edge prevents a well balanced stance. Your object then would be: first, to find a flat section of the teeing area, and second, to position the ball in relation to your intended target.

Most beginning golfers are unable to drive off the tee with enough finesse to avoid the hazard that may be located at the distance of an average drive. It is, therefore, wise to use the 3 wood for a shorter distance that avoids the area of the hazard.

Maintain consistency by playing your ball toward the fat (center) of the course. This entails keeping the ball in the center of the fairway and in the middle of the green, as well as progressing it toward the hole.

Where there is a dog leg in the fairway, a bend either to the right or to the left, you have two main choices: (1) To drive across the dog leg; or (2) to play it safe. In making your decision consider:

1. The distance it is to the dog leg.
2. Your ability to drive over the dog leg.
3. The advantage attained by driving across it.
4. Your approach to the green if you play it safe.

If, by cutting the corner of the dog leg, you are in a position for an 8 iron shot to the green in contrast to the 7 or 6 iron shot, there should be no hesitation. The difference is not worth the risk. The alternate route places your ball in a playable lie on the fairway with a direct approach to the green. Even though, in some cases, you will have to hit a wood or long iron with your second shot, your chance of landing on the green is greater than when you are forced to hit from behind the trees.

FAIRWAY

The second shot is often referred to as the "birdie maker" or the "pay off" shot. All strategy should be directed toward giving yourself every possible advantage. Since the fairway shot calls for accuracy and judgment of distance, it is sensible to hit the ball from a clean fairway lie, not out of a trap. Keep your ball in playing position at all times, and conserve your strength by staying out of traps and by aiming away from hazards.

When hitting from the rough, the effort should be directed to getting out with one shot. A beginner should avoid trying for the green, particularly if it calls for the very best shot. Not even a strong player, such as the current champions, can hit a good wood shot from tall grass every time. If you are in the rough near the green and have a clear view of the hole, then you have the advantage and may try for the green.

PUTTING

Even though putting involves the least effort of any shot during an 18 hole round, it is the part of the game that causes the greatest consternation. When you consider that 36 strokes are allocated to putting, you realize the importance of placing a ball in a position for an accurate stroke.

Since par figures for 18 holes are usually 70-74, you can readily ascertain that at least half of the strokes are awarded to the player who has developed skill approaching the green and putting. For this reason half of your practice time should be devoted to perfecting your short game.

When approaching, precision, not distance, is your main objective. The selection of the proper club can give you all the distance you need. There is, therefore, no reason to try to force a chip shot or an approach shot to gain more distance. Numerous strokes can be saved by developing the ability to place every short approach shot close enough to the cup to hole out in one putt.

Many traps will be methodically placed around the green. Should one be located between you and the hole, select the club necessary to carry (go entirely over) the trap or to land in front of it. Often, the players who win are those who place an approach shot in front of a trap and then chip over the trap for one or two putts.

When there is water or a trap behind the putting area, aim in front of the green and gamble on your chip shot to get you close enough to the hole for one putt. Greens that slope upward should be played short. In other words, aim for the area in front of the green. In this manner, you will have an uphill putt and a much better chance to keep the number of strokes low. A downhill putt that misses the hole will usually cost you more than one recovery stroke.

PRACTICE

Good golf is not learned on the golf course but on the practice ground. Once you have mastered the mechanics of the swing, you need to practice until the mechanics become second nature and to continue practicing so that you will stay "in the groove."

Light sessions of around 30 minutes create fun but do not reach the boring stage for the beginner. Some people spend a lot of time on the practice ground hitting balls, but never practicing. It is not the number of hours you put in on the practice area that counts but the way the time is spent. Have a purpose in mind. A common error is to stand there and hit balls with no thought of the swing, the target or the flight of the ball. Balls should always be directed at some area. The use of a target such as a tree or a chimney will create interest as well as providing a guide for judging your success or failure.

A beginning golfer should, first, master the basic shots from a good lie. If you can consistently repeat the same swing from good lies, you will have better control over the bad situations encountered during your games. Later as you become more skilled, vary your practice to include hitting balls from downhill lies, uphill lies, buried lies, over trees, out of sand traps and so forth. Practice on hitting out of the rough often helps to develop a beginner's game. To hit the shot you are forced to stay down longer and to swing the club through.

Work on your concentration, shutting out everything around you to the exclusion of where and how you want to hit the ball. Total concentration will not only help make your practice session worthwhile but will also develop your ability to concentrate on the course.

Develop a routine to your practice. Since golf involves a sense of timing and rhythm, start your practice session with putts to establish your rhythm and feel for the game.

Use every type of club during your practice session. Start with your putter and progress to the short irons. Select one club, the 9 iron for example and then skip every other club as you work toward your driver. The next time you practice, start with a different short iron. To give additional practice on your short game, finish with short irons and putting. An example would be:
1. putting
2. 9 iron
3. 7 iron
4. 5 iron
5. 3 iron
6. 4 wood
7. driver
8. 9 iron
9. putting.

GOLF IN STORMY WEATHER

Seldom does the weekend golfer find himself playing under adverse weather conditions; however, there are times when a sudden rain or windstorm comes up and your opponent wants to continue playing. During a club tournament you may also find yourself fighting the elements until play is canceled by the tournament committee. While the ability to swing correctly is certainly an asset, the more proficient player will have the versatility to adapt his game to un-favorable weather conditions.

Rain

1. Assume your stance on a section of the teeing ground that is not wet and slippery.

2. Tee your ball higher to insure proper flight.

3. Periodically clean your spikes with a golf tee or a similar object.

4. Allow yourself one extra club length for each shot. The ball will stop near the spot where it lands.

5. Par five holes are difficult to make; however, this is compensated by the fact that par three holes are easier.

6. Wet grass on the green tends to keep the ball on your putting line. In most cases, you may putt directly for the hole.

7. Keep the grips of your clubs dry. Wipe them with a dry towel. Leather grips are slippery if they become saturated with water. There is a new type of cork, rubber and linen grip which is water resistant and provides a firm grip in all varieties of weather.

8. Cloth gloves and a handkerchief wrapped around a leather grip will help you maintain secure contact with the club.

9. Wet weather keeps the ball low. On long fairway shots, use a 4 wood instead of a 2 or 3 iron.

10. Stop playing if there is an electrical storm.

11. Clean mud off the ball except when it is in a hazard.

Wind

1. Stroke lighter when the wind is behind you and harder if you are hitting into the wind.

2. Hit low shots directly into the wind. Widen your stance and place the ball back, closer to your right foot.

3. Allow for more roll on the ball.

4. Aim your ball to the left or to the right of your target when the wind is blowing across your line of flight.

6

Etiquette

Golf by its nature is a game in which good manners and consideration of others are imperative to an enjoyable round. A number of courtesies or rules of etiquette have been designed to make the match more pleasurable for both you and your opponents. Although there are general rules of etiquette accepted by golfers everywhere, each golf club has specific courtesies applicable to its course. Therefore, the first time you play a new course, study a copy of the local rules of etiquette or consult the golf professional or the person with whom you are going to play about the special rules.

FOR COMMENCING A MATCH

1. Arrive on time for your match. Plan your schedule in order to have sufficient time to park your car, get your clubs, secure a caddy and change your shoes.

2. Wear clothes which are appropriate for that particular course or country club. Some courses will require women to wear skirts and men to wear shirts (excluding polo shirts).

3. If you are a beginning player, you should avoid the more popular and thus crowded playing times of the week.

4. As soon as you arrive, register with the starter or club professional, pay your fees and obtain your starting time. Often the professional will have one of you place a ball near the first tee, behind the balls of other groups who registered previously. As a group tees off, its ball is removed. When your ball is first in line, your group drives from the first tee.

5. If you are planning to play in a twosome, the club starter may pair you with two other players. In this way more golfers are accommodated; however, if the course is not crowded, you will be allowed to play in a twosome.

6. As your starting time draws near, remain close to the first tee.

7. Before hitting your tee shot, check your ball to be sure that you will be able to identify it. Compare your ball with your partner's

and opponents'. If two of you have a ball with the same markings, volunteer to substitute another ball.

8. Offer the honor (driving first from the teeing ground) to your opponent; however, be gracious enough to accept the honor, if it is offered to you.

9. Delay your tee shot until those ahead of you have played their second shot and are well out of range.

10. When your partner or opponent is hitting a tee shot, stand facing him. On subsequent shots you should stand in line with the person hitting the ball. Avoid standing directly behind the person hitting a ball.

11. Remain quiet and motionless while your partner or opponent is addressing the ball.

12. As you hit a ball, watch it carefully until it stops rolling and then spot the position of the ball in relation to some permanent object on the course.

FOR THE FAIRWAY

1. Avoid delaying the game by studying your next shot and deciding on the club you will use as you approach your ball or while waiting for your opponent to play.

2. Allow the players behind you to play through if your group is playing slowly or if you are hunting for a lost ball.

3. When your ball lands in a sandtrap, enter and leave the trap from the lowest side. Ater leaving the bunker, you should remove your footprints and the club impressions by raking the area with a rake, located near the trap, or with your club.

4. Assist your partner and your opponents in spotting and searching for their balls.

5. Retrieve any divot you take and press it firmly into its original place.

6. Give a warning of "fore" if you think your ball may strike someone.

7. Wait until the players in front of you have left the green before hitting your approach shot.

FOR THE PUTTING GREEN

Proper preparation of the turf on the green is a carefully planned and expensive process. Club members, as well as the greenskeeper, take great pride in a green which enables a contestant to execute his putts to the best of his ability. Any scuff mark that you leave on a green is, consequently, a hazard to all those following you. The rules of etiquette, therefore, are strictly followed on the putting green.

1. When you approach the green to putt, place your golf cart and bag off the green, toward the next teeing ground.

2. Remove any mark made by your ball on the green by gently lifting the area with a golf tee and pressing the turf back into place.

3. Have a coin or ball marker available in order to mark the location of your ball upon request.

4. Be prepared to assist others in removing and replacing the flagstick. If your ball is nearest the hole, you should hold the flagstick. Place the flagstick on the ground beyond the putting green.

5. Avoid stepping or standing on your opponents putting line. If your opponent is in the process of putting, do not let your shadow fall across his putting line.

6. Walk carefully on the green to avoid damaging the putting surface with the spikes or the heels of your shoes.

7. When your ball lands on the wrong green, lift it and then drop the ball well off the green to prevent damage to the green and to the area immediately surrounding the green.

8. As soon as you have holed out, retrieve your ball from the cup.

9. After all have holed out, replace the flagstick and leave the green before recording your scores.

PRIORITY ON THE COURSE

1. When you are playing alone, you have no standing and must give way to any match.

2. When you are playing a complete match, you are entitled to play through any opponents who are playing a shorter round.

3. If you are playing in a twosome, you have priority over and are entitled to pass any threesome or foursome.

4. When your group loses more than one complete hole on the players in front, you must allow the match following you to play through.

Glossary

Ace—A hole made in one stroke.

Address—A position in which the player assumes a stance with his feet, body and clubface aligned in relation to the location of the ball.

Approach—A shot made with the intention of placing the ball on the putting green.

Apron—The closely cut area surrounding the green.

Away—The ball farthest from the hole.

Birdie—A score of one stroke under par for a hole.

Bogey—A score of one stroke over par for a hole.

Bunker—A depression, sandtrap or mound on the fairway.

Buzzard—A score of three strokes over par for a hole.

Caddie—A person who carries the clubs of a player.

Casual water—An unplanned accumulation of water on the golf course, not considered a water hazard.

Cup—The hole in the green into which the ball is played.

Divot—The piece of turf removed by the clubhead during a stroke.

Dog leg — A bend or curve in the fairway either to the right or to the left.

Dormie—A score in match play when a player or a side is as many holes ahead of an opponent as there are holes remaining to be played.

Double bogey—A score of two strokes over par for a hole.

Double eagle—A score of three strokes under par for a hole.

Down—The number of holes in match play or strokes in medal play a person is behind an opponent.

Eagle—A score of two strokes under par for a hole.

Fade—A ball in flight which moves slightly from the left to the right.

Fairway—The well mowed area of the course between the tee and the green.

Flagstick—A pole inserted in the cup to indicate the number of the hole and the location of the cup.

Flight—The divisions into which players are divided for a tournament.

Foursome—A group of four persons playing together who are competing against par or against each other.

Frog hair—The higher area of trimmed grass surrounding the green.

Green—The area of closely mowed turf surrounding the cup.

Halved—A tied score for a hole or a game.

Handicap—The difference between the average game of a player and par for the course. Also refers to a method of equalizing the playing ability of opponents by awarding strokes to the weaker players.

Hazard—A bunker or water trap strategically arranged to increase the difficulty of the course.

Hole out — The final stroke of a hole.

Honor — The side entitled to drive first from the teeing ground.

Hook — A flight of the ball which curves to the left.

Lie (of the ball) — The situation of the ball on the ground.

L.P.G.A. — Ladies Professional Golf Association.

Match play — A type of competition based on the number of holes won or lost.

Medalist — The person (or persons) who obtains the lowest score in the qualifying round.

Medal play — A type of competition based on the total strokes for the round.

Out-of-bounds — An illegal area, marked by a line or white stakes, which surrounds the golf course and on which play is prohibited.

Over-club — The use of a club which projects the ball past the intended target.

Par — A standard score established for a course or a hole, computed by determining the length of the holes and by allowing two putts for each hole.

P.G.A. — Professional Golf Association (Men).

Playing through — The courtesy of standing aside and permitting participants to play through a slower group.

Press — A shot in which a player attempts to apply more than his normal power.

Pull — A ball hit to the left of the intended line of flight.

Push — A ball hit to the right of the intended line of flight.

Qualifying round — A designated number of holes played prior to the tournament in order to ascertain eligibility and classification of participants.

Rough — The unkept area of grass which parallels the fairway.

Sand trap — A hazard on the fairway or around the green formed by substituting sand for topsoil.

Scratch player — A player who has a handicap of zero.

Shank — A shot in which the ball is contacted with the heel and the shaft of a club and projected at a right angle to the intended line of flight.

Slice — A stroke in which the ball curves to the right.

Smothered — A ball hit with a closed clubface. Ball will go into the ground immediately or will travel as little as 100 yards. If ball lifts off ground, it will hook. Clubface is closed so much it is called loaded.

Stance — The position of the feet in preparation to hitting a ball.

Stymie — A ball which has another ball or object directly in the intended line of play.

Tee — An object (usually wooden or plastic) used to elevate the ball for a drive.

Teeing ground — The starting area for each hole, usually designated by markers.

Threesome — A group of three persons playing together who are competing against par or against each other. One may play against the other two, each side playing one ball.

Topped ball — A shot in which the clubhead contacts the ball above the center line causing the ball to have a low flight or to roll along the ground.

Up — The number of holes in match play or strokes in medal play a person is ahead of an opponent.

U.S.G.A. — United States Golf Association.

Waggle — The short swings of a clubhead forward and backward used to relieve tension before striking the ball.

Water hole — A hazard of water strategically constructed and located between the tee and the green.

Whiff (fan) — A shot in which the ball is completely missed by the club.

Winter rules — The application of seasonal, local rules permitting a player to improve the lie of the ball on the fairway.

References

ANNOTATED BIBLIOGRAPHY

Wind, Herbert W.: The Story of American Golf. New York, Simon and Schuster, Inc., 1956. A comprehensive book on the history of golf in the United States from 1889–1956. Wind divides the history into six parts, presenting pertinent data on clubs and organization as well as biographical information on noted players.

Gibson, Nevin H.: The Enclyclopedia of Golf. New York, A. S. Barnes and Company, 1958. A thorough outline of golf in Europe and in the United States, with emphasis placed on tournament champions from 1888–1958.

Bowling, Maurene: Tested Ways of Teaching Golf Classes. Dubuque, Iowa, William Brown Company, 1964. A presentation of teaching procedures and progressions for beginning golf classes. Bowling's methods of instruction provide an insight into the world of golf and the problems encountered by beginners.

Player, Gary: Positive Golf: Understanding and Applying the Fundamentals of the Game. New York, McGraw-Hill Book Company, 1967. A book of special value to those who wish to engage in golf exercises and conditioning drills. A well illustrated discussion of the grip, the backswing, the downswing, the body position, timing and rhythm.

Grimsley, Will: Golf: Its History, People and Events. Englewood Cliffs, N.J., Prentice Hall, 1966. A thorough presentation of the origin and history of golf as well as biographical data on leading golfers of the past and the present. Grimsley also describes the origin and development of the major golf tournaments.

Browning, Robert: A History of Golf. New York, E. P. Dutton & Co., Inc., 1955. A detailed history of golf extending from the origin of golf in Scotland to 1955. Chapters focus on topics such as the game in America, championships, social customs, evaluation of the caddie and modern golf courses.

Rand McNally Golf Course Guide. New York, Rand McNally, 1966. A book length directory of more than 5000 golf courses in the United States, by the editors of Golf Digest. Each course is discussed and pinpointed on 19 sectional reference maps.

Charles, Bob: Lefthanded Golf. Pacific Palisades, Calif., Rose Books, 1972. A comprehensive, well-illustrated book on the left-handed approach to successful golf. Charles includes detailed instructions from the stance to course strategy and correction of errors.

FILMS

All-American Championship (collegiate), 1964, 1965, 1966. University of Houston, Dave Williams, Houston, Texas.

All Star Golf, 1957–1960. Miller Brewing Company., 4000 W. State St., Milwaukee, Wisconsin.

Buick Open, 1961–1966, including instruction by Lema, Burke, Collins, Boros, Hagge, Rodgers. Modern Talking Picture Service, 1212 Avenue of the Americas, New York, New York 10036.

Canadian Open, 1958–1966. Seagram's Distillers Company, Sales Promotion Department, 375 Park Avenue, New York, New York.

Great Moments in Golf. United States Golf Association, New York.

Masters, 1963, 1964, 1965, 1966. Travelers Insurance Company, Film Library, 52 Prospect Street, Hartford, Connecticut 06115, and Cadillac Motor Car Division, 2860 Clark Avenue, Detroit, Michigan 48232 (available through dealers).

Miller Open (men), 1957–1959. Miller Brewing Company, 4000 W. State Street, Milwaukee, Wisconsin.

Miller Open (women), 1962 — Miller Brewing Company, 4000 W. State Street, Milwaukee, Wisconsin, and Ideal Pictures, Incorporated, 417 North State Street, Chicago, Illinois.

PGA Championship, 1966 — Association Films, Incorporated, Ridgefield, New Jersey.

PGA Seniors' Teacher Trophy Golf Championship, 1964, 1965, 1966. Schieffelin and Company, Att. James Walsh, 30 Cooper Square, New York, New York 10003.

Shell's Wonderful World of Golf (33 films from television), 1964, 1965, 1966. Shell Film Service, 450 Meridian Street, Indianapolis, Indiana 46204 (central and east), or 430 Peninsula Avenue, San Diego, California 94401 (west).

St. Andrews, Cradle of Golf. United States Golf Association, 40 East 38th St., New York, New York.

U.S. Open, including:
"The Open: Triumph and Tragedy, Casper and Palmer at Olympic," 1966.
"The Open: Gary Player at Bellerive," 1965.
"The Open: Comeback of Ken Venturi," 1964.
"The Open: Ouimet and Boros at Brookline," 1963.
"Oakmont and the Open," 1962.
"U.S. Open Golf's Longest Hour," 1956.
"The Open: A Decade of Open Championships," 1960–1970.
"The Open: Tony Jacklin Conquers Hazeltine," 1970.
"The Open: Trevino at Merion," 1971.
All from United States Golf Association, 40 East 38th Street, New York, New York 10016.

Rules of Golf, Hazards. United States Golf Association, New York.

Walker Cup Matches, 1959. United States Golf Association, 40 East 38th Street, New York, New York 10016.

World Team Amateur, 1958, 1960, 1962, 1964, 1966. United States Golf Association, 40 East 38th Street, New York, New York 10016.

INSTRUCTIONAL FILMS AND LOOP FILMS

May be purchased or rented from The National Golf Foundation, 707 Merchandise Mart, Chicago, Illinois.

Purchase Rates — 16 mm Motion Pictures

Unit I Welcome to Golf	$45.00
Unit II Building Your Swing	95.00
Unit III Pitching, Pitch and Run and Sand Shots	45.00
Unit IV Putting	45.00
Unit V Courtesy on the Course	120.00
Complete Series	315.00

Rental Rates — 16 mm Motion Pictures

Unit I	7.00
Unit II	10.00
Unit III	7.00
Unit IV	7.00
Complete series	25.00

Rental Rates — 8 mm Loop Films

Loop 1	The Grip — The Address Routine	$19.95
Loop 2	The Full Swing — Woods and Irons	19.95
Loop 3	The Short Approach — Pitch-Pitch and Run	19.95
Loop 4	The Putt	19.95
Loop 5	The Sand Explosion Shot	19.95
Loop 6	Uneven Lies — Uphill, Downhill, Sidehill	19.95
Complete set		113.00

GOLF MAGAZINES

Golf. Universal Publishing and Distribution Corp., Canton, Ohio (monthly).

Golf Digest. Golf Digest Incorporated, Box 629, Evanston, Illinois (monthly).

Golfing. Golfing Publication Inc., 407 S. Dearborn Street, Chicago, Illinois (monthly).

Golf World (by subscription only). Golf World Company, Box 2000, Southern Pines, North Carolina (weekly).

Golf Course Superintendents' Association of America, 3158 Des Plaines Avenue, Des Plaines, Illinois.

Golfguide. Werner Book Corporation, 631 Wilshire Blvd., Santa Monica, Calif., (monthly).

The Lady Golfer. Seidal Publications, Inc., Box 118, Scottsdale, Arizona (10 times a year).

The Golf Journal. United States Golf Association, New York (8 times a year).

RESOURCE MATERIAL

National Golf Foundation, Room 804, Merchandise Mart, Chicago, Illinois.

SLIDES

Golf Rules in Pictures. Set of 35 mm slides of the basic rules of golf. $25 per set. United States Golf Association, 40 East 38th St., New York, New York.